BLACK PAPER

The Randy L. and Melvin R.
Berlin Family Lectures

BLACK PAPER

WRITING IN A DARK TIME

TEJU COLE

THE UNIVERSITY OF CHICAGO PRESS

Chicago and London

The University of Chicago Press, Chicago 60637
The University of Chicago Press, Ltd., London
© 2021 by Teju Cole
Published 2021
Paperback edition 2022
Printed in the United States of America

31 30 29 28 27 26 25 24 23 22   1 2 3 4 5

ISBN-13: 978-0-226-64135-5 (cloth)
ISBN-13: 978-0-226-82386-7 (paper)
ISBN-13: 978-0-226-64149-2 (e-book)
DOI: https://doi.org/10.7208/chicago/9780226641492.001.0001

Library of Congress Cataloging-in-Publication Data

Names: Cole, Teju, author.
Title: Black paper : writing in a dark time / Teju Cole.
Other titles: Randy L. and Melvin R. Berlin family lectures.
Description: Chicago ; London : The University of Chicago
    Press, 2021. | Series: The Randy L. and Melvin R. Berlin
    Family lectures | Includes index.
Identifiers: LCCN 2021016936 | ISBN 9780226641355 (cloth) |
    ISBN 9780226641492 (ebook)
Subjects: LCSH: Arts and society. | Art and society. |
    Photography—Social aspects. | Art and race. | Arts—
    Moral and ethical aspects. | Aesthetics, Modern.
Classification: LCC NX180.S6 C636 2021 | DDC 700.1/03—dc23
LC record available at https://lccn.loc.gov/2021016936

for Sasha

Contents

Illustrations

Preface

Black Paper address the fractures of our recent history through a constellation of interrelated concerns. Most of the essays in the book were written over a period of three years, beginning in late 2016. They explore a wide range of subjects: the color black in the visual arts, the role of shadows in photography, the consolations of music and architecture, elegies both public and private, and the complex links between political upheaval, literature, and activism.

At the heart of the book are the Randy L. and Melvin R. Berlin Family Lectures, which I was honored to deliver at the University of Chicago in the Spring of 2019. Those lectures, under the title "Coming to Our Senses," are published here for the first time, in slightly modified form. They argue for the urgency of using our senses to respond to experience, recognize epiphany, and reframe our ethical commitments.

Black Paper is an account of how I have sought out the help of photographers, poets, painters, composers, translators, voyagers, mourners, and mentors to apprehend the wisdom latent in the dark.

PART ONE

After Caravaggio

Michelangelo Merisi da Caravaggio, born in late 1571 in Milan, is the quintessential uncontrollable artist, the genius to whom normal rules do not apply. "Caravaggio," the name of the Northern Italian village from which his family came, reads like two words conjoined, *chiaroscuro* and *braggadocio*: harsh light mixed with deep dark on the one hand, unrestrained arrogance on the other. Raised in the city of Milan and the village of Caravaggio in a family that some say was on the cusp of minor nobility, Caravaggio was six when he lost both his father and his grandfather, on the same day, to the plague. He was apprenticed around age thirteen to Simone Peterzano, a painter in the region, from whom he must have learned the basics: preparing canvases, mixing paint, perspective, proportion. He apparently developed a facility for still-life painting, and it was probably while studying with Peterzano that he absorbed the pensive atmosphere of Leonardo da Vinci and great Northern Italian painters of the sixteenth century like Giorgione and Titian.

Caravaggio most likely first went to Rome in 1592. The reason

might have been his involvement in an incident in Milan in which
a policeman was wounded (the details, as with so much else in
his life, are foggy). It would be far from the last time he had to
get out of town. In Rome, it did not take him long to gain both
acclaim and notoriety, and by the mid-1590s his paintings had
settled into the styles and subjects we often think of as Caravag-
gesque: lutenists, cardplayers, a panoply of brooding androgy-
nous youths. Eminent collectors vied for his work, Cardinal Scipione Borghese and Cardinal Francesco Maria del Monte among
them. Success went to his head, or perhaps it activated something
that had always been there. His language coarsened; his drinking worsened; he got into fights often and was arrested multiple
times.

In 1604, Caravaggio was thirty-two. He already had behind him
a string of indelible masterpieces, made for Roman patrons and
churches: *The Supper at Emmaus*, *The Calling of Saint Matthew* in
the Contarelli Chapel, *The Conversion of Saint Paul* in the Cerasi
Chapel, *The Sacrifice of Isaac*, *The Incredulity of Saint Thomas*. By
that year he had also completed *The Entombment of Christ*, a work
of profound grief and astonishing achievement, even by Caravaggio's already high standards. But in his personal conduct, he remained reckless. "Sometimes he looked for a chance to break his
neck or jeopardize the life of another," writes Giovanni Baglione,
a contemporary and one of his first biographers. Giovanni Pietro
Bellori, a later seventeenth-century writer, tells us, "He used to
go out on the town with his sword at his side, like a professional
swordsman, seeming to do anything but paint." At lunch in a tavern one day, he ordered eight artichokes, and when they arrived,
he asked which were cooked in butter and which in oil. The waiter
suggested he smell them to figure out the answer himself. Caravaggio, always quick to suspect insult, sprang up and threw the

earthenware plate at the waiter's face. Then he grabbed a sword; the waiter fled.

As a boy in Lagos, I spent hours poring over his work in books. The effect his paintings have on me, the way they move me but also make me uneasy, cannot be due only to long familiarity. Other favorites from that time, like Jacques-Louis David, now seldom excite me, even as Caravaggio's mesmerizing power seems only to have increased. And it cannot only be because of his technical excellence. The paintings are often flawed, with problems of composition and foreshortening. My guess is that it has to do with how he put more of himself, more of his feelings, into paintings than anyone else had before him.

The themes in a Caravaggio painting might derive from the Bible or from myth, but it is impossible to forget even for a moment that this is a painting made by a particular person, a person with a specific set of emotions and sympathies. The maker is there in a Caravaggio painting. We sense him calling out to us. His contemporaries may have been interested in the biblical lesson of the doubting Thomas, but we are attracted to Thomas's uncertainty, which we read, in some way, as the painter's own.

But there's more than subjectivity in Caravaggio: There's also the way his particular brand of subjectivity tends to highlight the bitter and unpleasant aspects of life. His compact oeuvre is awash in threat, seduction, and ambiguity. Why did he paint so many martyrdoms and beheadings? Horror is a part of life we hope not to witness too often, but it exists, and we do have to see it sometimes. Like Sophocles or Samuel Beckett or Toni Morrison — and yet unlike them — Caravaggio is an artist who goes there with us, to the painful places of reality. And when we are there with him, we sense that he's no mere guide. We realize that he is in fact at home in that pain, that he lives there. There's the unease.

Late in May 1606, two years after the artichoke incident, Caravaggio lost a wager on a game of tennis against a man named Ranuccio Tomassoni. A fight ensued, in which several others participated. Caravaggio was injured in the head, but he ran his sword through Tomassoni, killing him. After two days of hiding in Rome, he escaped the city, first to the estates of the Colonna family outside Rome, and then, near the end of the year, to Naples. He had become a fugitive.

Caravaggio's mature career can be divided in two: the Roman period, and everything that came after his murder of Tomassoni. The miracle is that he accomplished so much in that second act, on the run. His work changed—the brushwork becoming looser, the subject matter more morbid—but he remained productive, and he remained valued by patrons. He worked in Naples, in Malta, in as many as three different cities in Sicily, and in Naples again before he set out for Rome in 1610, in the expectation of a papal pardon. He died on that return journey.

In the summer of 2016, I had plans to be in Rome and Milan for work. The US presidential campaign was proceeding with wall-to-wall coverage, and the body politic was having a collective nervous breakdown. The bizarre candidacy of Donald Trump had established him, against all odds, as a contender. Right-wing movements were gaining ground across the world. Fleeing war and economic distress, thousands of people were dying in the Mediterranean. The brutality of ISIS had made videos of beheadings part of the common visual culture. What I remember of that summer is the feeling that doom wasn't merely on its way; it had already arrived. (It had arrived, but then it evolved, and four years later, had become something else again.)

2

I knew I would revisit paintings by Caravaggio in Rome and Milan. At least he would tell me the truth about doom, and I would find in him the reprieve certain artists can offer us in dark times. And that was when an old and long-cherished idea came back to me: What if I traveled farther south, visiting each of the places Caravaggio had in his years of exile? Many of the works he made in those places remain, some *in situ*. Naples, Valletta, Syracuse, Messina, and possibly Palermo. The more I thought about the idea, the more I wanted to make it happen. I wasn't after a luxurious summer sojourn. The places of Caravaggio's exile had all become significant flash points in the immigration crisis, which was not entirely a coincidence: he'd gone to them because they were ports. A port is where a given territory is most amenable to arrival and to escape, where a stranger has a chance to feel less strange. I had two strong reasons for deciding to undertake the journey: First, I longed for the turmoil I knew I would feel in front of Caravaggio's paintings in the museums and churches where they were held. But second, I wanted to see something of what was happening at that moment outside, beyond the walls.

I arrived in Naples in late June, by train from Rome. It was my first time in the city, and the taxi driver, a middle-aged man, must have guessed as much. He explained that there was a fixed fare of twenty-five euros between the Napoli Centrale station and destinations in town. By the time the concierge at the hotel confirmed that the trip shouldn't have cost more than fifteen euros, the driver was gone. Later that evening, on Via Medina, half a block from my hotel, I passed by a woman sleeping on the ground. Most of her body was covered by a small blanket, but her feet stuck out, and I was reminded of the bare and dirty feet of the

Virgin Mary that had so offended the first critics of Caravaggio's *Death of the Virgin*. The next day, the sleeping woman was gone, but I saw another woman seated near the same spot, yelling at passersby in garbled words that were probably incomprehensible even to speakers of Italian.

Naples bookended Caravaggio's years of exile. The first visit was late in 1606, the second in 1609, and he undertook important commissions on both visits. By October 1606, he was already being plied with offers and welcomed into the highest Neapolitan artistic circles. One of his first completed works in Naples was for the recently formed charitable society of the Pio Monte della Misericordia. The painting, for which he was paid without delay and which he was quick to deliver, was a large canvas titled *The Seven Acts of Mercy*. It can be seen to this day in the church for which it was commissioned in the center of the city, just off the narrow Via dei Tribunali. *The Seven Acts of Mercy* is a complex painting that tries to compile into a single vertical plane seven distinct vignettes, allegorical counterpoints to the seven deadly sins. In reproduction, the picture seems a congested mess. But in real life, at more than twelve feet high in a small octagonal building, it is uncannily absorbing.

The protagonists emerge from pools of darkness to play their respective roles, and they seem to drop back into that gloom when the viewer's eye moves on to other sections of the painting. On the right side of the painting is an allegory of charity from ancient Rome: the elderly Cimon breastfed in prison by his daughter. A body being carried out behind her (we see only the feet) represents the burial of the dead. In the foreground, a bare-torsoed beggar, sprawled at the feet of Saint Martin, represents the clothing of the naked. *The Seven Acts of Mercy*, with its stacked narration as well as its light effects, was to have a sensational influence on Neapolitan painting after Caravaggio. This was something of a pattern for him: in each city where he lived, he was like a lightning bolt, a startling but brief illumination in whose aftermath nothing was ever the same again. When I came out of the church into Via dei Tribunali, *The Seven Acts of Mercy*, with its surging movement and sharp divisions of light and dark, seemed to continue on the busy street.

On the day I arrived in Naples, I saw some young African men selling shirts and hats just outside Napoli Centrale. That afternoon, I went down from Castel Nuovo to Castel dell'Ovo, where boys dived from the causeway into the bay. Near the entrance of the castle, a man sat selling trinkets. He was Senegalese and sometimes worked as a translator of books. He was fluent in French, Italian, and English. His current project, he said, was about the African presence in Italy. I asked him where the Africans were in Naples, and he said perhaps I'd find some at Piazza Garibaldi. But, he added, that was not a neighborhood I'd want to be in after nightfall.

That evening I wandered instead through the Quartieri Spagnoli, the crowded "Spanish Quarter," where Caravaggio lived and where he found the combination of high culture and low life that so appealed to him. The streets of the quarter were narrow, the buildings tall; many walls were decorated with graffiti. It was easy to imagine it as a place where life had been boisterous and cheerful for a long time, a place of concealment and informality — just the thing for a man on the run. The Quartieri Spagnoli was crowded that night, full of residents, students, and tourists. My server at the pizzeria where I dined, a jovial young man, had a tattoo on his arm: *veni, vidi, vici*. It was an allusion to Julius Caesar, of course, but it could also be, I later found out, an identifying mark among members of Italy's resurgent far-right movement, a sign of their nostalgia for Mussolini's fascism.

The next morning, I went up to the Museo di Capodimonte, located in the northern part of the city in a building that used to be the palace of the Bourbon rulers of Naples and Sicily. After a long, straight sequence of rooms, I arrived at Caravaggio's *The Flagellation of Christ* (figure 1). Christ stands at the column, life-size, and around him are three assailants, two of whom pull at him, the third of whom crouches, preparing a whip. As so often with Caravaggio, there is the story that is depicted, but beyond it, and often overwhelming it, is an intensification of mood accomplished through his use of unnatural shadow, simplified background, and a limited palette. It is an image of brutal injustice, an image that makes us ask why anyone should be tortured.

When I left the museum and walked down the Capodimonte hill, strolling through the busy city at evening, I was distressed. I imagined that I was being watched by people in the doorways and windows. I began to think about how Caravaggio, once he escaped into exile, could never take a good night's sleep for granted, but I was also thinking about all the people in the city at that very moment who were in one way or another precarious guests: the woman in the doorway at Via Medina, the man selling trinkets at Castel dell'Ovo, the many young Africans I saw at the train station.

Naples had given me two magnificent late paintings by Caravaggio, but my efforts to see a third had been thwarted. *The Martyrdom of Saint Ursula*, reputed to be his very last painting, was out on loan. I decided I would leave for Palermo the following day. I wasn't traveling in correct order: Caravaggio went from Naples to Malta, and only then to Sicily and eventually back to

FIGURE 1. Caravaggio, *The Flagellation of Christ* (1607). Oil on canvas. Museo di Capodimonte, Naples. Photograph: Wikimedia.

Naples. But my intuition was to leave Malta almost for the end, a remote culmination to a dream journey.

Night had fallen by the time I got back to my hotel room. Below me lay the city, its houses packed close in the dusk, their lights glittering like a cloud of fireflies all the way to the edge of the water with its ferries and cruise ships—beyond which lay, in almost total darkness now, the Bay of Naples, Mount Vesuvius, the Isle of Capri, and the Mediterranean Sea.

3

The Oratory of San Lorenzo on Via Immacolatella in Palermo is surrounded by a tangle of streets so narrow and twisty that I got quite close to the building without seeing it. I took two wrong turns before I finally found the entrance. On the high altar in the chapel of this oratory, Caravaggio's *Nativity with Saint Lawrence and Saint Francis* hung for centuries. Caravaggio is likely to have made the painting in 1609, though the somewhat conservative style (elements of the composition bring to mind his much earlier *Calling of Saint Matthew*), as well as the paucity of documents, put that date in doubt. What is certain is that the painting was made before 1610, and that it was one of the treasures of Palermo until the night of October 17, 1969, when it was hacked out of its frame by persons unknown, never to be seen since.

The consensus now is that the Mafia was most likely involved in the theft and almost certainly responsible for the final fate of the painting. What was that final fate? Stories have floated around. It was sold off; it was fed to pigs; it was burned in a fire. But nobody knows for sure. In its place now, on the high altar of the oratory, hangs a copy commissioned in 2009 and painted from photographs of the original, a plucky facsimile that looks nothing like an authentic Caravaggio. Perhaps this is why the printed tourist information asks visitors to cast their eyes elsewhere and enjoy "the beautiful marmoreal floor realized in 1716 by the artists of murble Francesco Camanlino and Alojsio Mira." But my pilgrimage was not to see a marble floor. Caravaggios are so few—around eighty are agreed upon by scholars—that the absences feel like scars: those mentioned by seventeenth-century writers that haven't survived or been identified, the three that burned in Berlin in 1945, the one that haunts the oratory in Palermo.

The summer of my trip was a difficult time in Italy, but Sicily had its own special difficulties. I couldn't be sure, for instance, whether the many examples of graffiti I saw with the word "ultras" referred to soccer fanatics, right-wing political thugs, or some combination of the two. In the heat of the afternoon, I walked through the Ballarò market, its gaudy stalls offering produce and cheap goods. When I returned, the sun was going down, and the city had undergone a change. The market's stalls were shut, the streets almost silent. There had been stories about the conflicts some Nigerians in Palermo had had with the Mafia, their involvement in prostitution, the terrible acts of violence they both endured and perpetrated, the stabbings and slashings. None of that was visible during my stroll through the Ballarò market that evening, but the vibe was tense, and I knew that I didn't want to stick around.

4

Two things were clear to me by the time I took a train the following morning along the Sicilian coast from Palermo — via Cefalù, Capo d'Orlando, Gioiosa Marea, and Barcellona, a succession of unfamiliar towns — to Messina. The first was that I could no longer separate my exploration of Caravaggio's years in exile from what I was seeing around me in contemporary Italy: the sea was the same, the sense of endangerment rhymed. The second was that, after my stymied attempt to see *The Martyrdom of Saint Ursula* in Naples and the predictable disappointment of seeing the replica *Nativity* in Palermo, I was more than ready to stand in front of a real and great Caravaggio painting again. I got into a taxi at the station in Messina. The driver said, "So, you're a football player?" I laughed. Indeed, what else could a young African headed to a hotel be? "No, I'm here to look at paintings by Caravaggio." "Ah, Caravaggio," he said, unconvinced. "Caravaggio. Great."

In Messina I met up with Alessandra Coppola, a Neapolitan journalist who had agreed to be my guide in Sicily. After lunch, we walked around the city, which was unlike any I had seen in Italy: modest, modern, full of flat-roofed multistory buildings devoid of ornament. There was a good reason for this: an earthquake leveled Messina in December 1908, destroying 90 percent of its buildings and killing more than seventy thousand people in the surrounding area. The city that emerged in the aftermath was plainer and more rational than many other Italian cities its size. Many of the new buildings were designed to withstand future earthquakes.

In the late afternoon, Alessandra and I went to the Museo Regionale di Messina, a simple building on a rise near the strait that separates Sicily from the mainland. There were trees and marble antiques scattered about its grounds. We were visiting on a Wednesday afternoon, and almost no one was there. We felt fortunate as we moved through the silent galleries. Stepping into a large gray room, without fanfare or warning I found myself standing before *The Raising of Lazarus* (plate 2). It hit me like a sudden gust of wind. I don't know if I cried out, but I know I began to shake. I approached it, making sense of it as I moved closer — a harshly lit, frightening picture, an entanglement of limbs, some as yet unresolved drama — and as I did so, I saw that there was a second painting in the room, also by Caravaggio: his *Adoration of the Shepherds.* This was a quieter work, but it was also large and had its own force field.

I sat on a bench in the middle of the room, the two paintings set at a right angle to each other. I was awestruck, out of breath, caught between these two immensities. The very act of looking at an old painting can be so strange. It is an activity that is often bound up with class identity or social aspiration. It can sometimes feel like a diverting, or irritating, stroll among White people's ancestors. It can also often be wonderful, giving the viewer a chance to be blessed by a stranger's ingenuity or insight. But rarely, something even better happens: a painting made by someone in a distant country hundreds of years ago, an artist's careful attention and turbulent experience sedimented onto a stretched canvas, leaps out of the past to call you — to call *you* — to attention in the present, to drive you to confusion by drawing from you both a sense of alarm and a feeling of consolation, to bring you to an awareness of your own self in the act of experiencing something that is well beyond the grasp of language, something that you wouldn't wish to live without.

The Raising of Lazarus, painted around 1609, is dominated by the dark expanse in its upper register. Below, as though spotlit, is the scene of resurrection. At the center, stretched out in a diagonal, taut between death and life, is the pallid, almost greenish body of Lazarus. A man supports him, and his sisters mourn on the right side of the painting. On the left is the figure of Christ, with his head backlit, stretching out his right arm to summon life back into the dead man. Golden light is flecked over hands and faces, arms and legs.

I've always been moved by the story of Lazarus as it is recounted in the Gospel of John. The basic shape of the narrative is recognizable and relatable: someone dies, and the heartbroken family pleads for their loss to be reversed. In the case of Lazarus, Christ is so moved by the family's grief that he interferes with the natural order of things and grants an exception like no other: he brings the dead man back to life. This makes it an exemplar of a kind of cosmic partiality, what we would all hope for at our most wounded and vulnerable. Caravaggio pins the scene down to its material facts: the confused faces of the onlookers, the downcast faces of the sisters, the necrotic body of Lazarus, the supernatural authority of Christ.

The drama that unfolds in *The Adoration of the Shepherds* is, by comparison, much quieter. What can one do with the stable where the infant Christ was born? Many artists cannot rise above the story's fairy-tale baggage, but in Caravaggio's hands, the narrative is brought alive again. The key, as usual, is his trust in realism: show what things look like, and the feelings will come. The painting is a pool of burnt umber, swirling around the placental red of the robes worn by the Virgin and one of the shepherds. This is no sweet family scene, but rather a document of roughness and need. Why should a newborn and his mother be in such a dirty place, barely protected from the elements? What corner of a refugee camp is this? Why do these people not have a home?

Caravaggio left Naples in 1607 and ended up in Sicily in late 1608, taking commissions in Syracuse, Messina, and probably Palermo. But between his time in Naples and his arrival in Sicily, he spent more than a year farther south, in Malta. He had to leave Naples for reasons that are not clear. Then, Caravaggio being Caravaggio, he had to escape from Malta after committing a crime there. And when he left Sicily, it was inevitably in a hurry, this time because he feared for his life. He went from Sicily back to Naples, and then began to make his way toward Rome. He was productive in those convoluted final years and months, but he was also harried and homeless. It isn't hard to imagine that when he painted *The Adoration of the Shepherds*, he might have found himself in deep sympathy with the Holy Family. They were, after all, confronted with one of the simplest and most complicated of all human needs: a safe and decent place to spend the night.

5

At the hotel in Messina, I read in that morning's *Corriere della Sera* about a boat that sank more than a year earlier with seven hundred people onboard. That boat had now been retrieved by the Italian coast guard. It had been raised and was being taken from the sea to the Sicilian port of Augusta. I decided I would go to Augusta and watch the berthing of the boat. We departed from Messina and drove down the coast, past Taormina and Catania, on a clear bright morning that had Mount Etna's smoky peak visible on our right for long spells. The town of Augusta, when we reached it, was bright and deserted. We had lunch at a cafe there but could not find any information about the retrieved boat. So we drove farther down, past Syracuse, all the way to the southern tip of the island, to the resort town of Pozzallo. There was heavy traffic as we made our way through the town. A hearse went by, tailed by a large crowd on foot.

At the beach in Pozzallo, we met up with some Italian and American friends and then drove into the port area, where ferries and container ships usually docked. The gates were open, but there was no one at the window and no one else on the grounds. Between the dock and the road, fenced in behind the port area, and sitting on the parking lot some fifty yards away from us, were eight large wooden boats. Painted blue, white, and red, they were crammed up close together, each tilted to one side, several leaning against one another. I left my companions behind and began to walk toward the boats. Orange life jackets covered the decks and spilled out from them, and by the time I reached the boats, the strong smell they emanated had become a stench. The boats seemed to have been dragged in from the sea with no attempt made to clean them. They were festooned not only with huge quantities of dirty life jackets but also with plastic water bottles, shoes, shirts, and all the filth of many days of human habitation at close quarters.

There was no way of telling which, if any, of these boats had tipped its human cargo over into the Mediterranean, which had been intercepted by European authorities, or which had brought terrified travelers safe to shore. I had my notebook with me as I walked among them, and I made notes of what I was seeing. I observed the details, wondering how I might set it all down in writing. What happened next took me by surprise: I suddenly collapsed to my knees and began to sob. My chest pulsed, my tears flowed, and between those boats with their strong smell of human bodies, I buried my head in my hands, ambushed and astonished by grief.

When I regained my composure, I climbed into one of the boats, unbothered now by the stench, wanting only to be there, imagining the unseen and desperate crowd of seafarers. Then, after a while, I rejoined the group. We drove out of Pozzallo and returned to Augusta. It was a provincial port, full of cranes and ships and containers, much busier and much more extensive than Pozzallo's. There was a large fenced-in area set aside with tents for people who had been picked up within the last few days or weeks and who were awaiting processing and transfer to other sites. A large ship with many passengers was supposed to come in. We were now told it would not dock that night.

But a smaller group of migrants had arrived during the day, and a police officer gave me permission to speak with two of them. I was led to a room with bright fluorescent lighting. The men were Bangladeshi, both young, probably in their twenties. They looked dazed. They'd been given clean clothes—a checked button-down shirt for one, an athletic T-shirt for the other—and on their feet they wore plastic Crocs. They presumably spoke Bangla. There was an interpreter, a Pakistani man who was fluent in Urdu. He could get the general idea of what the men were saying, I assumed, possibly because they also knew some Hindi, which overlaps appreciably with Urdu. But there was another problem: this interpreter spoke fluent Italian but only halting English. And so, there was work involved in getting him to understand my questions and further work involved in him getting the Bangladeshi men to understand his interpretation of my questions. When they finally understood something of his questions and responded, there were the same number of imperfect steps to get the answer back to me.

The men were both named Mohammed. One of them was bigger than the other. They had been rescued from a boat coming from Libya, where they had been living and working for more than a year. Why did they leave Bangladesh? To find work, they said. And how had Libya been? Big Mohammed shook his head. It was very bad, he said, they had to get out of there, the Libyans were cruel; but it cost a lot of money to gain passage on the boat. And how was the journey? Again, it was big Mohammed who answered: The traffickers had lied, he said. The passengers were told they would be in Italy in six hours. But they were out at sea for almost an entire day before they were picked up by the Italian ship.

I asked them what they hoped to do, and it was the smaller Mohammed who spoke up now. They wanted the freedom to work in Europe, he said. His companion nodded in agreement. Their fatigue was apparent—the fatigue of having just that day survived an ordeal at sea. That's what I kept thinking about: that they had lived but others had died. Why had things turned out that way? It was a matter of luck, and this seemed to contribute to their bemused air.

We were told of another boat that was to dock later that night, at a second and smaller port in the Augusta area, a few minutes' drive away. The large ship we had expected, we were now told, had been prevented by the authorities from docking. But a handful of its passengers were to be brought ashore for emergency medical attention. And so we went to this other port, and after half an hour, a small covered boat did indeed come in. There were other members of the press present on the pier with us, and we were all allowed to witness the boat's docking but not to get close to it or to take pictures. Police officers patrolled the area while six or so medical professionals, clad in white full-body protective gear and white face masks, boarded the boat. Soon, they lifted out a frail man and placed him onto a stretcher. He was wheeled over to the ambulance. One of the Italian journalists suggested he was Eritrean.

Not long afterward, the medical professionals in their white suits and masks led a Black couple, a man and a woman, out from the boat, and then a second couple. Both women were pregnant. Each of the four was helped off the boat and onto the pier and then led up the pier to the waiting ambulance. I went up to the ambulance. One of the men was seated near the door, and I asked him where they were from. "Nigeria," he said. Feeling that I was somehow overstepping my professional bounds, but also imagining that perhaps these people would not hear many soft words in the coming days, I said, "Welcome." Then I added, "God be with you." Before the man could respond, a police officer closed the ambulance door and waved me from the area.

6

Syracuse is built of a honey-colored stone, the same stone used for humble homes as well as for the cathedral dedicated to the city's patron saint, Saint Lucy. Her legend is typical of female Christian saints: a vow of chastity, consecration to God, defiance of the temporal authorities (in her case the governor of Syracuse), and subsequent gruesome execution. Versions of the legend say that Lucy's eyes were gouged out before she was executed. Saint Lucy is the patron saint of the blind, and in her statue atop the cathedral, she holds a dish in which she carries her eyes.

A contact in Syracuse had put me in touch with a young man from Gambia who came across by boat from Libya some eight months earlier. D. had registered as a minor — he admitted to me that he was no longer one, and I put his age at about twenty — and he had been placed in a group home with other minors. He had a dark and intelligent face and an easeful manner that reminded me of my younger cousins. He seemed glad to be speaking English to someone and was even happier when I told him I was Nigerian. "I love Nigerian music," he said. "It's all I listen to." I asked him why he migrated. His father had been a small-time politician, he said, and had fallen afoul of Gambia's then president, Yahya Jammeh. "My father was forced into exile in Dakar. Things were very difficult for my family. For my mother, for my sisters." But why didn't D. also move to Dakar? "I wasn't so close with my father." But then his father died, and the situation became even more desperate. He went to Libya, to find work there, and managed to send small sums home. When he at last decided to pay money to human smugglers for a passage to Europe, he told no one back home.

"You weren't afraid of dying?"

"I was, a little," he said, "but Libya had become bad. I had to go."

It was the same story, in essence, as that of the Mohammeds. "And the journey, was it as bad as you feared?" "Worse," D. said. The smugglers had given a radio to one of the passengers, whom they arbitrarily appointed "captain." The instructions were that he try to contact one of the Italian ships after a certain period of time. After a few frantic hours, the stratagem worked, and the migrants were picked up and taken to Sicily. Only on arrival did D. let his family know he had even attempted the trip. He said the Italians had been kind to him. He was still living in the house for minors, where he had a certain amount of freedom. But he had very little money and no working papers. Months had passed, and he was now itching to leave Syracuse and go to a larger city.

Then he asked me why I was in Syracuse. I told him I was there to see a painting by Caravaggio. I pointed toward the Piazza Duomo and asked if he would like to accompany me. He said he didn't see why not. As we entered the church of Santa Lucia alla Badia together, he said, "You know, I come around here every day, around this piazza, and I've never been inside a church. Not this church, not any church. In my whole life, I mean. I've never seen the inside of a church." He was raised Muslim. He seemed amazed that he could just walk in, that no one questioned his presence or stopped him at the door. We went to stand in front of the altarpiece.

The Burial of Saint Lucy is enormous, at ten feet across and more than thirteen feet high. It is in poor condition now: the paint surface is abraded, and large areas are damaged. But this does not weaken the effect of the painting. If anything, the material frailty of the image helps focus your attention on its funereal mood. Saint Lucy, dead, is stretched out on the ground, a cut visible in her neck, her eyes sealed shut. A crowd has gathered behind the body. In the foreground, two powerful-looking men dig into the ground, but this "ground," lost in a field of dark browns, makes it seem as though time itself were burying the picture. Darkness encroaches on the protagonists from all sides. As D. looked at the painting, I wanted to tell him about how Caravaggio, by this point in his travels, was quite paranoid and had taken to sleeping with his sword. But I didn't. We looked at the painting together for a while, and then we stepped out of the church. Outside, D.'s eyes seemed full of wonder, as much from Caravaggio, I supposed, as from me, this strange fellow West African who appeared out of nowhere, asking odd questions.

7

From the air, the first impression I had of the largest of the Maltese islands was of a large corkboard floating in the sea: a flat brown terrain set off from the water by vertiginous cliffs. On the drive in from the airport, the taxi driver offered, unprompted, "Malta is nice, but we cannot feed all these refugees. We are a small island. We are not a big country." Malta is distinguished by well-preserved homes and churches, the imposing fort of Castel Sant'Angelo, and the lasting and omnipresent influence of the Sovereign Military Hospitaller Order of Saint John of Jerusalem of Rhodes and of Malta. It was the patronage of this militant Christian organization, also known as the Knights of Malta, that drew Caravaggio to Malta in July 1607.

Caravaggio lived in Malta for a little over a year and in that time made a small number of paintings for the Knights, whose patron saint is Saint John the Baptist. His stiff, dutiful portrait of Alof de Wignacourt, the grand master of the order, hangs in the Louvre. Another portrait of Wignacourt is presumed lost. These paintings were probably made to curry a specific favor: to get him into the good graces of Wignacourt, so that Wignacourt would grant him a knighthood, to improve his chances of a papal pardon for his murder of Tomassoni. The island still has two major paintings from Caravaggio's time there. The first is *Saint Jerome Writing*. The second is the work that, more than anything else, took me to Malta: *The Beheading of Saint John the Baptist* (plate 1), a painting I had known about since I was a boy, well before I had any idea of Malta as an actual place.

The most populated part of Malta is a dense agglomeration of towns near Valletta, the capital. I stayed in Sliema, one of those towns, dined by the waterside, walked in the quieter streets, wandered. It wasn't until the third day that I plucked up the courage to go to the Co-Cathedral of Saint John in Valletta. The co-cathedral (so called because the old Maltese capital, Mdina, in the interior of the island, already had a cathedral) is gilded and ornate and pulses with the murmur of visitors. But if you follow the signs, passing through a small door at the back, you enter a small, quiet, chapel-like room, the oratory. Straight ahead, but visible only after you come around a fixed partition, is *The Beheading of Saint John the Baptist*. The effect is of having walked in on something horrible, something you wish to unsee.

The seven people depicted in the painting feel like real people in a real space, dwarfed by the dark background. The lighting, the monumental scale (even larger than *The Burial of Saint Lucy*), the height at which the picture is hung, and the distribution of dark and light all add to the impression that what you are seeing is an actual event: the two prisoners watching the execution; the servant girl with the gold plate; the old woman; the man directing the killing; the executioner reaching for the knife with which to finish the job; and Saint John himself, prostrate on the floor, his neck spurting blood. Caravaggio signs his name below, the only time we know him to have done so, with a red line drawn out of that blood.

All the malevolent force of the paintings by Caravaggio I had seen in the preceding two weeks — *Judith Beheading Holofernes, The Martyrdom of Saint Matthew, David with the Head of Goliath, The Flagellation* — all that murderous power seemed now to have been distilled into a single nightmare image, a surveillance camera trained on an unfinished crime, a snuff film.

The Beheading of Saint John the Baptist was difficult to absorb into my understanding of whatever it was I thought painting was. More than a year would pass before I found a key that helped me process what I saw in Malta: two brief video clips from Libya made in 2017. The first, filmed by an unnamed source, shows men being sold at a slave market. The second was made by CNN journalists who went into the suburbs of Tripoli to confirm the story. The men being sold are migrants from Niger, a few of them standing at night against a bare wall, a desolate courtyard like that in Caravaggio's painting. The light is poor. It's hard to see. The business is brisk and rapid: prices are called out, unseen buyers bid, and it's over. In those clips, what I saw was life turned inside out, life turned into death, just as I had seen in Caravaggio's painting. Not simply what ought not to be, but what ought not to be seen.

The painting impressed Caravaggio's hosts. On July 14, 1608, not long after his completion of the painting, he was named a Knight of the Order of Saint John. Alof de Wignacourt made the proclamation, comparing him to Apelles, the greatest painter of ancient times. Caravaggio was awarded a gold chain and, according to Giovanni Bellori, Wignacourt "made him a gift of two slaves." Most of those enslaved in Malta were Muslim, at a time when the hatred between the Knights of Malta and the Ottoman Empire was at a mutually fanatical pitch (there were many enslaved Christians in the Ottoman lands). We don't know the identity of the two people handed over to Caravaggio, but many enslaved people who worked in a domestic context in Malta were from Bornu, which spanned parts of present-day Nigeria and Chad.

Caravaggio did not get to enjoy his cruel status for very long. By late August, he was involved in yet another violent fracas. Giovanni Rodomonte Roero, a high-ranking knight, was wounded one night in an assault, and Caravaggio and five other men were implicated. Caravaggio was held at Castel Sant'Angelo for weeks. But he somehow escaped from captivity, lowering himself from the fort with a rope. Finding a boatman, whom he may have bribed, he made straight for Sicily. Thus came Syracuse, Messina, Palermo, the great paintings he made in those months trailing him like so many bread crumbs; and then, feeling he was under mortal threat in Sicily, perhaps fearing the reach of the Knights of Malta, he returned to Naples, to another spell of productivity in a city he knew well. He thought he would be safe in Naples. He was mistaken. In October 1609, on his way out of a tavern, he was surrounded by a group of men. They beat him up and slashed his face. It has been suggested that he was partially crippled and partially blind after the attack. It took him a long time to convalesce. Between that assault and the end of his life, a nine-month period, he produced no more than a handful of paintings, the last two of which are believed to be *The Denial of Saint Peter* and *The Martyrdom of Saint Ursula*.

Less than a year after I went to Naples, the Metropolitan Museum received *The Martyrdom of Saint Ursula* on loan. I was able to see it side by side with *The Denial of Saint Peter*, which is in the Met's collection. Because we know he died not long after, we cannot help reading these paintings through the lens of a late style, as works that convey both the tremendous skill of the artist and his sense of hurry. They are paintings of great economy and psychological depth. The fear in Saint Peter's eyes, the grief on Saint Ursula's face: was this the insight of a man who knew his life was almost over? It's tempting to think so. But Caravaggio expected to recover from his injuries of the previous year. He expected a pardon from the pope. Even with a substantial body of work behind him already, he was only thirty-eight. He must have thought he was just getting started. He wasn't moving from life into death, like John the Baptist. He was moving from death back into life, like Lazarus. So he thought; so he hoped.

In the summer of 1610 Caravaggio received word that a pardon was being arranged for him in Rome, with the involvement of his old patron Cardinal Scipione Borghese. He left Naples on a felucca, a sailing boat, in the middle of July, taking three paintings with him as presents for the cardinal. A week later, he was in Palo, a coastal fort town twenty miles west of Rome, from which he presumably planned to make his way to the city. But something went wrong in Palo. On disembarking, Caravaggio got into a scuffle with the officers of the fort and was arrested. The felucca set sail without him but with his paintings still on board. It headed north to the coast of Tuscany, to the small town of Porto Ercole. Possibly there was another passenger to drop off. When Caravaggio was released, days later, he hurried overland in the direction of Porto Ercole, a day's ride. Upon arrival, he collapsed in an exhausted heap. The felucca arrived around the same time.

It was a hot July day in 2016 when I headed to Porto Ercole. My train from Rome passed by Palo after about thirty minutes and arrived in Orbetello–Monte Argentario an hour and a half later. I imagined it could have been a fever-inducing journey in July 1610. I stayed in Orbetello and took a taxi from there the following morning, across a spit of land that ends in the promontory of Monte Argentario, on the southern side of which is Porto Ercole. I had breakfast at a cafe on the rocky beach. A quartet of visitors was seated near me, two of them, from their accents, American. One American was an older man. "Well maybe this guy will win the election, and he can put an end to all that," he said. "Political correctness is just crazy. You're not even allowed to compliment anyone anymore. They'll cry sexual harassment." He held forth with the attitude of one who wished to be overheard. He complained about his ex-wife. His three companions nodded sympathetically.

Caravaggio never painted the sea. I search his oeuvre in vain for a seascape; vistas of any kind are rare. We can address only what has survived of his work, and in what has survived, there are no swells, no waves, no oceanic calms, no shipwrecks or beaches, no sunsets over water. And yet his final years made a chart of the sea, and his ports of call were all literal ports, portals of hope, of which Porto Ercole was the final, unanticipated stop. He's buried somewhere there, perhaps on the beach, perhaps in a local church. But his real body can be said to be elsewhere: the body, that is, of his painterly achievement, which has gone out to dozens of other places around the world, all the places where wall labels say, "d. 1610, Porto Ercole."

He was a murderer, a slaveholder, a terror, and a pest. But I don't go to Caravaggio to be reminded of how good people are, and certainly not because of how good *he* was. To the contrary:

I seek him out for a certain kind of otherwise unbearable knowledge. Here was an artist who depicted fruit in its ripeness and at the moment it had begun to rot, an artist who painted flesh at its most delicately seductive and its most grievously injured. When he showed suffering, he showed it so startlingly well because he was on both sides of it: he meted it out to others and received it in his own body. Caravaggio is long dead, as are his victims. What remains is the work, and I don't have to love him to know that I need to know what he knows, the knowledge that hums, centuries later, on the surface of his paintings, knowledge of all the pain, loneliness, beauty, fear, and awful vulnerability our bodies have in common.

I walked down to the harbor in Porto Ercole. Small boats in their neat dozens bobbed on the water, and I asked one of the waiting men to take me out. The air was clear, the water a deep blue with faint hints of purple. For the second time on my journey, I got into a boat. We zipped along, and when the boatman took his shirt off, I did the same. He seemed to be in his early fifties, and he said he had always lived in Porto Ercole. He spoke little English. When I told him I was from New York, he grinned and gave me a thumbs up. "Oh, New York!" he said. We were a couple of miles out. Did he know of Caravaggio? Of course he did. He pointed to the beach. "Caravaggio!" he said, still smiling.

I signaled to him to cut the engine. It sputtered to a stop, and the silence came rushing in, so that the only sound was that of the waves lapping at the hull as the boat rose and fell on the Mediterranean.

PART TWO

ELEGIES

Room 406

1

Alas! Sha'del, the son of Zabdibôl, the son of Moqîmu, the artisan. He died on the 3rd day of Kanûn (in) the year 484 (November, 172 CE).

2

The destruction of a ruin is like the desecration of a body, a vengeance wreaked on the past in order to embitter the future. And how often it is that those who destroy ruins are the same ones who desecrate bodies.

3

I need to understand what I am sad about, not in hopes of obliterating the sadness, but in hopes of lessening it.

4

Underneath modern Tadmor was Tadmor Prison. The dungeon was built for horror. The population was in the thousands. To keep the population fearful, random prisoners were dragged to death, or cut to pieces with an axe. Above stood the ancient ruins. The Syrian poet Faraj Bayrakdar, held at Tadmor Prison from 1988 to 1992 for his communist ideas, called it "a kingdom of death and madness."

5

Alas! Tadmor, the wife of Moqîmu son of Nûrbel, the artisan. She died on the 29th day of Siwan in the year 457 (June, 146 CE).

6

I displace what hurts, what cuts, onto some other object charged with a local pain from ages ago. The mourners and the ones they mourned are eighteen centuries gone. Their pain—"Alas!"—remains fresh.

7

The way the women raise their right hand to touch, delicately, the hem of their robes. Their irises incised, their pupils doubly incised, into the limestone.

8

Alas! Nûrbel, the son of Moqîmu (son of) Nûrbel. In (the month of) Qinyan of the year 492 (July, 181 CE).

9

There are two other people in Room 406. One of them is a young man in a black T-shirt and black shorts. The museum will close soon. Outside is the city. It is late in the afternoon and summer is almost over. Many languages flow through the streets, many people, and the UN building is a marine green in the August light.

10

On June 26, 1980, a putsch against President Hafez al-Assad fails. The Muslim Brotherhood is deemed responsible. The next day, commando forces, under orders from Rifa'al al-Assad, the president's brother, go to Tadmor Prison with orders to kill every prisoner, whether they are connected to the Muslim Brotherhood or not. The commandos arrive at dawn. The prisoners are in their cells, and the commandos go from one cell to another. No records are kept, but about a thousand prisoners are believed killed.

11

The ancient city of Tadmor (a possible etymological link with the Arabic *tamr*, "dates," is unproven), an oasis in the Syrian desert for millennia, becomes, under Greco-Roman influence around the first century CE, Palmyra (the name evokes date palms). Underneath Palmyra, Tadmor persists: the local dialect of Aramaic, carved into limestone stele as "Palmyrene," the Arab queen Zenobia, who fights, and wins, and loses, and is carried off to Rome in chains of gold.

12

Parthian (later "Persian") dress, Greek style, in this place where cultures meet (figure 2). The faces are frontal, both idealized and stylized, and responsive to second- and third-century CE Roman portraiture. The simplified folds of the robes fall like palmate leaves. The snicks of Palmyrene script are dry fronds.

13

That repeated "Alas!" tells it how it is. The amphitheater was built during the Roman imperial era. In our time, people are lined up

FIGURE 2. Anon., funerary relief (ca. 2nd–3rd century AD). Limestone. Palmyra, Syria. Photograph: Metropolitan Museum of Art, New York (Purchase 02.29.1).

in the amphitheater and shot. One notable horror of ISIS is that the individual dies as part of an unnumbered mass. No one knows how many have been killed, how many raped, how many made to disappear from earth without the dignity and rites that might lessen grief. Two hundred? Two thousand? Twenty thousand? How many people have been murdered during ISIS's deranged campaign to reinvent the world? What were their names? Who did they love? Who were their parents?

14

Not "art," vaguely. Not "archaeology," imprecisely. But rather: this specific object, that specific object, what it looks like, what it means. What it is to look at it on a particular day, and reiterate our debt to its custodians. As a sometime historian of art, I feel like a member of this complicated tribe of caretakers. How many of us were killed by the Baath regime before the war? How many archaeologists, historians, and art historians were killed in the American bombing of Baghdad? How many carvers, how many oud-makers, how many masters of the maqam, how many singers? How many of those who cherish the past on behalf of the future? Who is in charge of keeping the tally?

15

The young man in Room 406, in his black shirt, black shorts, black shoes, and black socks, goes from case to case with rare attention. He plays nervously with his hands, but his face is serene.

16

The ruins and tombs of Palmyra were in the protective custody of the old professor. A distinguished archaeologist, esteemed scholar, and member of the Baath Party since 1954, he was destined to die once the city fell. Professor Khaled al-Asaad was taken to a dungeon — not Tadmor Prison, which ISIS had already destroyed — but elsewhere. Here in this city he had loved and protected, they tortured him. Best not to imagine what happens in a torture chamber to a man of eighty-two. Then they killed him. And that is just the beginning, alas.

17

In a few minutes, Room 406 will close for the day. The carving, a fine blend of the Hellenic and the Persian, is distinctive: no other art looks like this. The rich merchant families of Palmyra sustained this art. Some of the stele are half-length busts; others, more complex, show a reclining figure attended by a number of other figures. In high relief, the figures are smaller than half life-size, and are arranged around the grave, as in a Roman dining room. In the world to come, we will be at banquet together.

Mama's Shroud

When my grandmother, my mother's mother, died in late June 2017, I sought out photographs of her. She'd died in Nigeria while I was in Italy at a conference. I wasn't with her when she slipped into a coma or, three days later, when she died. When my brother told me the news, I called my mother and other members of my family to commiserate with them. She was buried within a day of her death, according to Muslim custom, and I couldn't attend her funeral. My mother, visiting friends in Houston, had also missed the coma, the death, and the funeral.

I opened up my computer and began to search my folders for pictures of my grandmother. On each yearly trip to Nigeria for the previous several years, I had gone to see her in Sagamu, the small town some forty-five minutes north of Lagos in which she was born and in which she'd lived for most of her life. On these visits, she would say, "Sit next to me. I want to feel your hands in mine. Be close to me. I want your skin touching mine." I was always happy to sit with her, and to hold hands with her. Afterward, I took photos. I have photos of her alone, in selfies with me, in the company of my mother and my aunts. In these photos, she has surprisingly smooth skin, hardly any gray hair, and, in most of them, a trace of amusement. One pair of images shows my wife Karen holding her aged hands and painting her nails.

To remain close to our dead, we cherish images of them. We've done so for millennia. Think of the Fayyum portraits, which show us the faces of ancient Egyptians with stunning immediacy. Think of Palmyrene sculpture. Images — paintings, sculptures, photographs — remind us how our loved ones looked in life. But in most places and at most times, a visual memento of how people really looked was available only to a society's elites. Photography changed that. Almost everyone, now, is captured in photographs, and outlived by them. Photographs are there after people pass away, serving both as reservoirs of memory and as talismans for mourning.

My grandmother was born in 1928. Her given name was Abusatu, but we called her Mama. Mama's father Yusuf had been a stern imam in Sagamu, and Yusuf's father Ladani was reputed to have been even more severe. But Mama herself was serene and good-natured, kind, and tolerant. She was deeply consoled by her religion but not doctrinaire about it. Of her five daughters, three (including her first born, my mother) married Christians and converted to Christianity. It made no difference to Mama. The family had Muslims, Christians, and some, like myself, who drifted away from religion entirely: Mama loved us all equally. An example of her unobtrusive compassion: while I was a college student in the US, she sent me a white hand-woven cotton blanket. I never knew why, and didn't ask. But it is to this day the most precious piece of cloth I own.

I was leaving Rome when I received the sad news of Mama's death. She was approaching eighty-nine. The end had come swiftly, and she had been surrounded by family. One could say it was a good death. But why couldn't she have lived to ninety-nine, or to a hundred and nine, or forever? Death makes us protest the fact of death. It makes us wish for the impossible. I could objectively understand that I was lucky to have had a grandmother in my forties, and that my mother, sixty-seven at the time, was fortunate in having had a mother so long. My father was six when his mother died; he's been mourning her for almost as long as my mother's been alive. But the grieving heart does not care for logic, and it refuses comparisons. I mourned Mama as I left Italy for New York.

I mourned her but did not, or was not able to, weep. The flight landed in New York in the late afternoon, perhaps around the very moment Mama was being interred. My mother had forwarded a couple of photos taken by my cousin Adedoyin to Karen's WhatsApp. Karen reached for her phone and showed me the pictures. They were a shock. One was of Mama, dead on her hospital bed, wearing a flowery nightdress and draped in a second flowery cloth, the oxygen tube still taped to her nostrils. Her right arm was limp at her side; she was not quite like someone asleep, but rather like someone passed out, open and vulnerable. The other photograph showed a figure wrapped in a white shroud, tied up with white rope, laid out on a bed: a bundle in vaguely human shape where my grandmother used to be. I burst into sudden hot tears.

What did these photographs open? Imagination is delicate. It imposes decorum. A photograph insists on raw fact, and confronts us with what we were perhaps avoiding. There she is, my dear Mama, helpless on the hospital bed, and I cannot help her. Days later, I would find out from my mother that in this first photograph, Mama was still in a coma and not dead yet. But looking at the second photograph, the one in which she's incontrovertibly dead, my thoughts had raced through a grim logic. I thought: why have they wrapped her face up? Then I thought: it must be stifling under that thing, she won't be able to breathe! Then I thought: she's dead and will never breathe again. And that was when my tears flowed.

Mama's life had been hard. An itinerant trader of kola nut, and later the owner of a small provisions shop, she was one of my late grandfather's five wives, and by no means the best treated of them. She never went to school, and the only word she could write was her name, sometimes with the "s" reversed. But when Baba died more than twenty years ago, Mama moved out of his house and lived in the two-story building her daughters built her. She was a women's leader, a kind of deaconess, at the local mosque. She went to parties, to market, and to evening prayers. She lived in the security of her own house, in the company of her widowed second daughter, my aunt. In those later years, life became easier.

"She has a single obsession," my mother used to say, "and that's her burial rites." Mama insisted that she be buried the same day she died, whenever that day came. "She'll say, 'And I must not be buried at the house,'" my mother said, "'because what's rotten must be thrown out. And for seven days, food must be cooked and taken to the mosque and served to the poor.'" Most importantly, my mother said, Mama would reiterate that in a cupboard in the room next to the meeting room in her house was her robe, the one she must be buried in. It was of utmost importance to her to meet her maker wearing the robe in which she had approached the Kaaba, the holiest shrine in Islam.

The Hajj, the pilgrimage to Mecca, which she undertook in 1996, when she was sixty-eight years old, had transfigured my grandmother. Through that journey, through her accomplishment of one of the central tenets of Islam, she had sloughed off her old life and taken on a new one, one that put her into a precise relationship with eternity. The year of her journey, thousands of Nigerian pilgrims had been turned back due to a cholera outbreak. My grandmother was one of a few hundred who got through. When she returned from Mecca, many of her townspeople took to calling her "Alhaja Lucky." And as though to fit the name, she wore the serene mien of someone who was under special protection. My mother, an Anglican Christian, had financed the journey, knowing what it would mean to her mother to fulfill this final pillar of the faith. But, possibly, she'd had no idea how much it would mean. She'd anticipated the social satisfaction Mama would get from it but had not counted on the serious existential confirmation it provided.

In the last few years, I often thought of Mama's pilgrimage robe. I thought about how fortunate she was to have something in her possession so sacred to her, something of such surpassing worth, that she wished to have it on when she met God. And she had her wish: beneath the plain white shroud in which she was sheathed after she died was that simple pilgrimage robe.

I look at the various photographs from Mama's last years on my computer. None of them wholly satisfy me. Many are blurry, most are banal. I only really like the ones of her hands: they remind me of her wish to have her hands touched by mine. But the photograph I cannot stop thinking about is the one my cousin took, of Mama in her funeral shroud. The image reminds me of newspaper photos of funerals in troubled zones in the Middle East: an angry crowd, a shrouded body held aloft. But Mama was not a victim of violence. She died peacefully, well past the age of eighty-eight, surrounded by family.

Nevertheless, the custom is connected. It is a reminder that the term "Muslim"—so much a part of contemporary American political argument, and so often meant as a slur—is not and has never been an abstraction for me, or for millions of other Americans for whom it is a lived reality or a fact of family. A lead headline in the *New York Times* just a few days after Mama's burial read, "Travel Ban Says Grandparents Don't Count as 'Close Family.'" The headline was about the ban on visitors from six predominantly Muslim countries. Nigeria was not yet on the list—as it would later be—but the bald prejudice and cruelty it conveyed, not to mention the pointed absurdity of defining family to exclude grandparents, felt only too real.

On the night of Mama's burial, I lay down to sleep in my apartment in Brooklyn. I couldn't shake the image of my cousin's photograph. I went into the closet and took out the white cotton blanket Mama had sent me all those years ago. It was a hot night, high summer. I draped the blanket over my body. In the darkness, I pulled the blanket slowly past my shoulders, past my chin, over my face, until I was entirely covered by it, until I was covered by Mama.

Four Elegies

TOMAS TRANSTRÖMER

In Tomas Tranströmer's 1970 collection *Night Vision*, there is a poem called "A Few Moments" (many of his poems have laconic titles), translated by Robert Bly. The final section of the poem gets into my bloodstream:

> It is as if my five senses were hooked up to some other creature
> that moves with the same stubborn flow
> as the runners in white circling the track as the night comes
> misting in.

There is a sense of helplessness in Tranströmer, the sense of being pulled along by forces external to yourself. Movement as well as inadvertence. The long line here, the subclauses building, the full meaning of things taking shape additively, like huge white clouds, can almost be read in one breath, but not quite. It's more like a breath and a half, or maybe two full breaths:

> *It's as if my five senses*
> *were hooked up to some other creature*

that moves with the same stubborn flow . . .

(— this feels about a breath long to me. But then it continues . . .)

the same stubborn flow
as the runners in white
circling the track
as the night comes misting in.

That's a second full breath. Both inhabit this single sentence. Few sentences answer so many questions with such simultaneous economy, amplitude, and mysterious exactness. Just before each question, the line could stop and still be good. But it moves on, extended by its elaborations, growing associatively but not predictably, making syntactically visible the stubborn flow it describes, full of extraness but not excessiveness. The senses, the creature, the flow (precisely *stubborn*), the runners (precisely in *white*, like corpuscles), the track, the night, the mist. Circling the track: it goes on and on, coded with a "repeat" command. And how medical all of it is, but nowhere saying so.

It's as if my five senses were hooked up to some other creature (that does what?) that moves (how?) with the same stubborn flow (as what?) as the runners in white (doing what?) circling the track (when?) as the night comes misting in.

Tired in all five of my senses, life goes on, circling the track. I sleep for ten hours, and dream of Tranströmer.

I. M. PEI

In 1984, *Le Figaro* called I. M. Pei's design for the Louvre "soulless, cold, and absurd," and it wasn't alone in its vituperation. *Le Monde* hated it, too. One poll said 90 percent of Parisians opposed the design. A chief complaint was that Pei wasn't French. People did not necessarily separate their opposition to the design from their astonishing racism against the architect. There were horrifying caricatures of Pei in the French papers: a buck-toothed Chinaman destroying French culture.

I often think about the racist aspect of that opposition. But the dogs bark, the caravan passes. Pei's career was monumentally successful despite the racism, and the building is of course beloved, now. But also, no one should have to endure such.

The solution Pei arrived at was a simple geometric volume in the Cour Napoléon that would admit natural light into an underground passageway. Clear glass, specially made to a rare level of transparency, would flood the cavern with light. A dream of lightness amid all the depressing old stone. The capping volume would be a transparent dome, perhaps, or a square. No: a pyramid.

"The building is of course beloved, now." The bold modernism of the Pyramid is something I've always enjoyed: successful not only because of how different it is from its palatial sixteenth- (and nineteenth-) century environs, but because of how similar it is, genetically: the geometry, the rhythm, which despite the glass and steel and aluminum, evokes classicism. But what it evokes even more obviously is Egypt. And there the questions arise: questions of a Pyramid at the Louvre, of the enormous Egyptian art collection inside the museum itself, of the Luxor Obelisk at the Place de la Concorde. There are questions of theft, colonialism, and White supremacy. Pei's Pyramid contributed to that generations-long debate uncritically.

No one who dies famous at 102 does so without being a bundle of contradictions. I like the East Building of the National Gallery, and I have a fond personal memory of the JFK Library, without loving the building. I like thinking of how many people's happy memories are tied to the Pyramid at the Louvre. But I find most of Pei's buildings unexciting. Bland office towers and massive high-rises were not a tangential aspect of his career or success. With the benefit of hindsight, I much prefer the sensitivity to material and responsiveness to vernacular form that comes through in the work of architects like Wang Shu and Lu Wenyu. But perhaps that's unfair, since Wang and Lu are of a much younger generation. One should in any case love buildings, not architects. The age of the single great man of architecture is over, and collaboration must now be recognized. And yet, some men were great.

KASSÉ MADY DIABATÉ

In the early part of the previous century, in the environs of Kéla, some sixty miles south of Bamako, Mali, villagers would troop out to hear a djeli named Mady Diabaté (Mady is a local contraction of Mohammed). Mady's voice was so expressive that his hearers were moved to tears. They eventually bestowed on him the name "Kassé Mady," Bambara for "weep Mady": Mady, the one who makes others weep. Mady Diabaté's grandson, born in 1949, was given the same name: Kassé Mady Diabaté. It's one of those wondrous things: they knew the boy would become a singer, would continue the familial trade. But how did they know *his* voice would bring his own future hearers to tears? And yet, I wept listening to Kassé Mady's voice before I knew what the name meant.

The younger Kassé Mady's controlled baritone could soar, but it was especially moving when it stayed level, gently modulated. You would feel in your body the way the note values were cleanly stretched, not loud, and then the way the final note of a phrase would crumble, weeping in order to make you weep. (Listen, for instance, to "Sadjo" from the sublime 2015 album *Kiriké*.) Over the years I've been much comforted by Kassé Mady's close relationship with the djeli tradition, the way his Mandé ancestors' language and storytelling live through him, and the sustained otherness — other to conventional American reality — of his diction and vision. We are indebted to every instance of creative achievement that sidesteps the insistence of monoculture. Voices like Kassé Mady's, or Kandia Kouyaté's, or Salif Keita's, literally give us more life.

How marvelous it was to see Kassé Mady perform in New York with the kora master Toumani Diabaté in 2010. What noble and majestic men, restoring to us whatever those words could still mean. To be surrounded in that concert by people who knew and could feel the continuity and rootedness of Kassé Mady's cadences, and who praised him as the vessel of that language, was to be elevated and transported.

In his career, Kassé Mady was a treasured collaborator, working with the likes of Taj Mahal in the American blues tradition and Jordi Savall in the European early music tradition. "Tunkaranke," from *Kulanjan* (1999), the Taj Mahal collaboration, is an effective showcase for what was remarkable about his voice. Equally moving is a rendition, with his all-acoustic ensemble, of "Simbo," from the *Kiriké* album.

Kassé Mady Diabaté joined his ancestors in May 2018, at the age of sixty-nine.

ARETHA FRANKLIN

"And all through my coffee break time."

But why is that the line that pricks me? Because it is the most unaffected sentiment set in the realest of contexts. What is implied in "coffee break time" is that this is wage work. She punches in and punches out. She gets an hour for lunch, maybe fifteen minutes for coffee. I imagine this is a job in service. She needs the money, and there isn't that much of it. She runs for the bus, dear. While running she thinks of us, dear. Written by Hal David and Burt Bacharach, but sung by Aretha, spun into emotional gold by a girl who runs for the bus.

"At work I just take time . . ." Time that she doesn't have, a luxury she's not afforded but on which she insists anyway. Just a girl who loves a boy, you know? A boy she prays for, because to pray for someone is to love them further. 1968. The boy's in Vietnam. History bears down on the human heart.

The difference between Aretha's and Dionne Warwick's earlier version? Two greats, but there is sheer spare capacity in Aretha's voice. Dionne Warwick is minding herself, but Aretha's out on a lam. (She also benefits from a better arrangement, the piano given a more prominent role.) You can always feel how much extra she's got in the tank, you sense that she could be doing this faster and louder and stronger if she wanted, without losing an iota of control. Doing cartwheels on the tightrope. Aretha! Ms. Franklin had enormous power and dazzling range, of which Ms. LaBelle was the only real rival, and Whitney and Mariah the most serious inheritors.

Power. Spun light as air.

Two Elegies

In Memoriam Bisi Silva. In Memoriam Okwui Enwezor.

O. shows up in my dream last night. He is standing there as though listening to something. Wearing a dark, beautifully cut suit as usual. There's a great look of concentration on his face. He says nothing but, finally, he takes off his jacket. He folds it carefully, sets it down.

. . .

When I hear the terrible news that B. has died, I write to her right away, before I can stop myself, before I can talk myself out of the absurdity of writing to the dead. There's immediately an automated out-of-office reply.

. . .

How many of us loved them both. Our captains. Equal to each other. Unrivaled among the rest. They were proud of us? We were much prouder of *them*.

. . .

As in, all deaths are singular. To the one who dies and to those who love them, these things are not together. As in, when we go, we go alone. Grieve alone. Grieve singly. In the singular. But also . . . what? What is "together"? What is "singly"? Or "grieve." What.

. . .

Death's only lesson: we die.

. . .

Berlin, *The Short Century*, 2001. Venice, *La Biennale*, 2015.

. . .

O. writes of the "fractious memory of a time lived in the shadow of subjection and born in the deeply unethical code and moral conduct of colonialism." Back then I didn't even know one could write such things.

. . .

B. aged fifty-six. O. aged fifty-five.

. . .

B. writes of her intention "to strengthen programmatic, curatorial, artistic and discursive parameters of photography in dialogue with the international community." Which she did.

. . .

K'ójó pé sí'ra, we say in Yoruba. Or *ojó á jìnà s'ójó o*. Slightly different ways of saying the same thing: "May the days be far from each other." This is consolation in my mother tongue—the prayer or wish that bereavements, unavoidable though they be, will at least be mercifully spaced out.

. . .

Her crown jewel: the Center for Contemporary Art, Lagos.

. . .

B. dies on February 12, 2019. J. writes to me on February 23, 2019, in our mutual consolation: *ọjọ́ á jìnà s'ọ́jọ́ o.* O. dies on March 15, 2019.

. . .

Death's only lesson: we lived.

. . .

From B., I learned resistance. From O., I learned persistence.

. . .

Insufficiently distant days. And the things we still need to learn from you.

. . .

The students in Addis Ababa, drawn from all over the continent, how they loved B., and how they adored her for what she could teach them. In Venice, O.'s dazzle and what it was to feel a part of what he was, what he achieved on the biggest stage. We saw the criticisms, of course, we knew what *that* was all about, can't fool us. Public memory, private memory, Lagos, New York. The missed connections: Bamako, Munich.

. . .

Memory: meeting L., who had just returned from visiting O. in hospital. Her eyes puffy from crying.

. . .

An obituary is different from a lament.

. . .

From B., the scintillating possibilities in the local, a local never less than global. Her refusals. How this tilting-against-the-given became a refuge for me. From O., how to move in a room full of sharks. Man like a scalpel.

. . .

Bamako, *Recontres de Bamako*, 2015.

. . .

An admired figure, a friend, a dear friend, a family member, a confidante, a partner. A mild wounding a substantial wounding a derangement an impossibility. All the varying intensities of relation that seek a name in the aftermath.

. . .

Death's only lesson: no one knows what death's only lesson is.

. . .

C. overseeing the mortuary arrangements for O., his own grieving postponed.

. . .

Anne Carson's frequently cited lines from *The Glass Essay*:

> You remember too much,
> my mother said to me recently.

Why hold on to all that? And I said,
Where can I put it down?

. . .

Death sets off a flurry of reading and writing. Of rereading. How come so-and-so feels so alive in my inbox? What is the last email so-and-so wrote to me? Archive fever.

. . .

"Help me teach these young people how to write. They can't write!" Wrote B.

"I am so proud of you and all that you bring to literature, the world of ideas, and your insight into cultural practice in general. I continue to read your work avidly." Wrote O.

This is not an obituary.

. . .

"Comparisons are odious": a usage attested as far back as the fifteenth century. But, in contrast, the Igbo proverb that Achebe was fond of citing: "Where one thing stands another will stand by it." Sometimes there are two griefs (or more). It is death that is odious.

. . .

B. cites the griot Kouyaté: "I teach kings the history of their ancestors so that the lives of the ancients might serve them as an example, for the world is old, but the future springs from the past."

. . .

From O., how to deal with Europeans: skeptically. From B., how to deal with Africans: perseveringly.

. . .

R. doing memorial work, her mourning looking for an exit now, like someone in a dark room, hands tracing over the walls, not yet able to find the door.

. . .

An obituary is for the public, a lament is for the community.

. . .

Daudet in *In the Land of Pain*:

> The clever way death cuts us down, but makes it look like just a thinning-out. Generations never fall with one blow—that would be too sad and too obvious. Death prefers to do it piecemeal. The meadow is attacked from several sides at the same time.

. . .

"The dead" as a category—into which I am reluctant to admit either of you. The lament is an obituary that has forgotten its manners. Where can I put it down? Like a jacket removed and folded and set down. The future springs from the past.

. . .

In loss's dumbfoundery, *k'ǫ́jǫ́ pę̈ s'íra.*

A Letter to John Berger

You liked stories, so I'll tell you one. This happened in the Maniototo, in the central part of New Zealand's South Island, as the sun was dropping behind the Hawkdun mountain range, an undulating orange line, darkness below.

Inside the house the light is failing. Milo is eleven years old. Held, he cocks his head, as though he's listening for something from the mountains in the distance. He is perfectly still. I asked the man who holds him, "How did you know he was going blind?" The man says, "He began to bump into things more often."

White fur has grown over Milo's eyes, and his head now looks like an unfinished plush toy. He's been completely blind only a few months. Placed down, he runs around the house. He has a memory map of the house plan. Feathers are attached to the corners and legs of the furniture, so that he collides with hard edges less frequently. The soft white fur covers Milo's eyes, the soft white feathers tremble in the dark.

You're no longer here, John. No, let me say it plainly, even if it sounds harsh: you're dead, and death (as everybody knows) is final. But, nevertheless, I write to you as though you might be able to read this, as though you were only in hiding. The reason? Because of you!

Some years ago, when we were in conversation in Ferrara, I asked you about the dead. You peered out into the audience and said, "They are here with us. I believe that. They are helping us!" You said this with such conviction that I couldn't doubt it at all. And you meant not "the dead" as a general category, but as a group of highly specific individuals one has known and loved.

I was in New Zealand for two weeks. I don't know if you ever went there, but I thought of you a lot. It seemed that each person I encountered there had been touched by death: the deaths of children, spouses, siblings. *Et in Arcadia ego*, as Poussin called his famous painting. And yet, curiously, in each case I sensed that the dead were cohabiting with the living, and being cared for by them.

You once wrote: "For both hunters and hunted hiding well is the precondition for survival. Life depends upon finding cover. Everything hides. What has vanished has gone into hiding. An absence — as after the departure of the dead — is felt as a loss but not as an abandonment. The dead are hiding elsewhere."

When I got the terrible news that you'd died, it felt to me like a sudden darkness. But, John, since then, I've been discovering a fragment here, a passage there, a drawing over there, signs of you around the world, and these are like feathers you've thoughtfully placed in the places where we meet.

I know you're only hiding.

A Quartet for Edward Said

Edward Said loved music, and I loved his love of music, as well
as the musicality that characterized everything he did. I once saw
him at 116th Street in New York, when we were both at Columbia University. I was going into the subway, and he was pausing
ever so briefly outside its entrance, at the street crossing. This was
the word made flesh, the books in human form. I now wear from
time to time a beautiful suit, but back then, impoverished student that I was, it was beyond my imagination. So, I admit what
I first noticed was the suit. I was awed by the flash of glamour, a
glamour present each time I caught sight of Said's noble figure
on campus.

I first saw New York in 1975, when my parents were taking me
home to Nigeria from my birthplace in Michigan. This would
have been a transit stop, en route to London for a few weeks,
and then to Lagos. But I first knew New York in 1992, on my return journey to the US as a teenager. The city I arrived in, the
day after the Fourth of July, had a general reputation for violence,
with nearly two thousand murders that year (lately the number
is in the low hundreds), and had, that morning, a specific hang-

over from the previous night's patriotic celebrations. The streets were filled with trash, streamers, bottles. It was a Sunday morning, and few people were about. The memories are fleeting. My father, who traveled with me on that occasion, had pointed out a man taking food out of a rubbish bin: "That's America. Nothing is to be taken for granted here. You understand?" A few days later, we got on a train and, leaving New York, made our way to Michigan, which was considerably more tranquil.

Beethoven's String Quartet no. 15, op. 132, his thirteenth to be written but the fifteenth to be published, tempts one to agree with the strange notion that there is such a thing as pure music, music better than any possible performance. It's a romantic idea, and it's probably not true, since music exists in the hearing, not on the page. But listening to Beethoven's Op. 132, or Op. 130, or Op. 135—or for that matter Schubert's D. 960, or his Quintet in C, or Brahms's Clarinet Quintet—you can see why people think so. Within the written tradition of Western classical music, as in all genres of music, there is music that exhausts superlatives.

Op. 132 begins with understatement, a misty and sweet attitude. The marking is *Assai sostenuto—Allegro*, and it enters with an unresolved four-note motif. Softly, like something emerging on delicate legs from a fog. There is melody, or a fragment of a melody, beautiful, hesitant, as though it could bolt at any moment. This is music that in its tonality does not seem unrelated to Schoenberg. Slowly, the notes gather, like careful animals at first light.

I first truly knew New York in 1995. That winter I had returned from some months in Scotland and stayed with an uncle in Hackensack, New Jersey. I commuted into the city every day to an internship at a financial firm in Downtown Manhattan, at the World Financial Center. The World Financial Center was connected by a skyway to the World Trade Center, and every evening, on my way to Penn Station to catch the bus that would take me back to the suburbs, I walked across the skyway and passed through the World Trade Center. In the below-ground section of the World Trade Center in those days was a Tower Records. The record shop had listening posts, where I would while away a half hour or so on many evenings, listening to classical, jazz, or what used to be unironically called "world music." One evening, I placed the headphones on my head, and heard for the first time the third movement, the *Poco allegretto*, from Brahms's Third Symphony. The recording was by Claudio Abbado and the Berlin Philharmonic. For more than six minutes, I stood there, transfixed. I felt I had never heard such a thing before, nothing that was both so full and so tender.

I first really knew New York in 2000, after I finished my master's degree in London and began a PhD at Columbia. New York was fast and hectic. It had certain charms, but it was dirty, and too expensive, and not particularly safe. I was unhappy my first year in the city, and sure I wouldn't stay long, but, with familiarity, my feeling began to change. Then, after September 2001, a completely different intimacy emerged in my relation to the city, the intimacy of having been present with others during a disaster. Out of this intimacy, this feeling for the city, a few years later I began writing a novel, which, right from the beginning, I titled *Open City*.

I never stay very long in one place. I have known half a dozen cities as home. But I arrived in New York at the beginning of the century and lived there for eighteen years. I stayed, longer than I ever stayed anywhere. It was from New York that I started to properly imagine the wider world, and it was from New York that I set out into these worlds.

I still listen to that Brahms recording. It has a ravishing kind of beauty, immediately understood as supremely intelligent but also accessible. Not long ago, I was in a taxi, listening to it, and was surprised to find myself passing the site where the World Trade Center towers had stood: a remarkable coincidence. The towers, of course, were gone. But the music—music one would have thought of as delicate and helpless—was still blooming out, and it always will.

When I saw Said at the crossing at 116th Street, what I saw was a tall man with eyes so vivid they seemed lined with black. He had a distracted air, like one dreaming several worlds into being. He was in the world, he was in many worlds at once. I didn't dare say a word to him. (Or did I say hello? I honestly do not remember now.) He waited for the traffic to pass so he could cross the street, as though he were late for something but unworried about it.

The first movement of Op. 132 becomes gradually established. Established, but never quite coherent. Many different gestures are presented, only to be abandoned: march-like, aria-like, cadenza-like, gavotte-like. The musicologist Susan McClary compares this rapid catholicity of invention to John Cage's randomly alighting on different stations by intermittently spinning a radio dial. Within recognized conventions, an immense changeability is explored. This idea. That idea. Another idea. Yet another idea. It is an uncontrollable and slightly manic fecundity. Adorno writes, "The caesuras, the sudden discontinuities that more than anything else characterize the very late Beethoven, are those moments of breaking away; the work is silent at the instant when it is left behind, and turns its emptiness outward."

One evening in the late fall of 2006, I sat down and began to write the novel. It is narrated by a young psychiatrist named

Julius who lives in New York City during and in the years after the September 11 attacks. As he walks around the wounded metropolis, he finds himself doing a kind of emotional archaeology of the city. In the middle of the book, he travels to Brussels, a kind of double for New York: a center for the European imperial idea, as New York is a center for the American imperial idea. And in his desultory journey to Brussels, ostensibly undertaken to find his German grandmother, who had been a war refugee in Berlin, Julius meets some strangers. Most notable among them is a young man named Farouq, a Moroccan intellectual who works in a phone shop. They fall into deep conversation over the course of several days.

2: RAMALLAH

Beethoven was in terrible pain between 1824 and 1825. He was sick, with some kind of gastrointestinal trouble. His doctor put him on a regimen that forbade wine, coffee, and spices. The doctor also advised him to get away from the city. He moved to Baden, terrified that this illness was his death, come to him at the age of fifty-four. And inside that illness, he began to write a string quartet.

I recall the day Raja Shehadeh took us walking in the hills outside Ramallah. This was in May 2014. We left the congested city, went by winding mountainside roads, and soon were in the most incredible landscape, hills full of olive groves. The leaf of the olive tree is a matte green on one side and a silvery white or very pale green on the other. When the wind rustles a grove, you feel you are hallucinating. Everything feels alive, and looking at the trees there in their dozens, you suspect that they are about to rise into the air like a flock of birds.

In the Ramallah hills what is to be remembered is not omnipresent as it is elsewhere in the West Bank. The hills are a respite. But nothing has been forgotten. The elderly Christian woman in Birzeit who said, frankly, that she would never again see the sea, the sea she had grown up with, to which they had gone every summer. She is not forgotten. The people at the Qalandiya checkpoint, decent people who wish only to feed themselves and their families, who face daily humiliation and a monumental waste of time, subjected to interrogation and surveillance and the point of the gun, made to carry identity cards that have nothing to do with their identities. They are not forgotten.

The men and women working in the market in Hebron, Al-Khalil, where the settlers throw filth and urine and shit down from upper-story apartments and attempt to run them down on the roads, while bewildered young soldiers of the IDF patrol the area and permit every atrocity. They are not forgotten. And the stones, those bits of crystalized possibility, those symbolic gestures of re-fusal, scattered like auguries outside the inspection post, where daily the young men in uniform disrespect women old enough to be their grandmothers. These are not forgotten. The regime of permits and walls and checkpoints and prisons, the systematic eviction of families from West Jerusalem and from East Jerusa-lem, the judicial perversion of Ottoman-era paperwork in order to dispossess the rightful Palestinian inhabitants of Sheikh Jarrar who have been there for three generations, in favor of Hasidic Jews from Brooklyn; the refusal of entry to Palestinians living in exile, keen to see once again the beloved country. None of that is forgotten.

We had walked up the gentle slope of the Ramallah hills, and Shehadeh, who had been our host in the city earlier that day, had sat down on a rock. We had sat down around him, and to our surprise, he had begun to read from his book, *Palestinian Walks*, which was in part about walking in the Ramallah hills. Our eyes filled with tears.

Throughout his sickness in the spring of 1825, Beethoven worked on the new string quartet, the one that was to become his Op. 132. The uncertain and abstracted feeling of the first movement gives way to the second movement, which is characterized by a rustic feeling, like being out in the open air. I think of Bruegel's peasants. There's something both regular and irregular about their dance, and something both heavy-footed and fleet. When I told my friend Nilanjana I was thinking about Op. 132, she said this second movement was "a minuet whose melody can't really be hummed at all." She is right. It is just elusive enough that one can't quite settle into it. Perhaps its irregularity is meant to evoke the fluctuations of a fever.

In the middle of that second movement is a surprising but still rustic subject that sounds uncannily like a tune played on the bagpipes. As an undergraduate, I was an exchange student at the University of Aberdeen, and this is the music of those days. It is Scottishly folkloric, like a foreshadowing of Mendelssohn's *Hebrides Overture*. But it is choppy, unlike Mendelssohn. As Adorno wrote, it is characterized by "sustained tension, unaccommodated stubbornness, lateness and newness next to each other."

Palestine never let Edward Said go, and Edward Said never let Palestine go. His longing for Jerusalem, where he was born, and for Gaza, and the West Bank, and the '48, and all of Palestine, was the engine of all his work. He could give the wisest and most subtle reading of Gérard de Nerval or Richard Wagner, or he could be at the Lebanese border throwing stones toward an Israeli guardhouse, earning the admiration of those who loved humanity and the opprobrium of those who knew nothing; and through it all, it was Palestine that made his heart beat. And because he provided a language for it, and an undimmed determination for it, he helped open the eyes of many of us who were not Palestinian by birth or tribe or residence.

Farouq, when he and Julius first meet, declares that Edward Said means a great deal to him, because Said understood how hesitant Westerners were to accept difference. "Difference as orientalist entertainment is allowed," Farouq says, "but difference with its own intrinsic value, no. You can wait forever, and no one will give you that value." Later in the novel, there are long conversations between Julius, Farouq, and Farouq's closest friend, Khalil, conversations with stops and starts, with things misheard and misunderstood, with the ebb and flow of real argument. I wanted a conversation made of fragments, like the conversations we have in real life. I wrote these passages not to assert a particular political position — that is not, in my view, the role of novels — but to admit into the novelistic form a number of positions seldom articulated in novels. I wanted to push beyond the easy and acceptable liberal positions and reflect some of what I actually heard around me among people of conscience. At one point, Farouq declares: "Julius . . . I think you should understand this: in my opinion, the Palestinian question is the central question of our time."

Said described late Beethoven as "immobilized and socially hesitant." Adorno had gone further. For him, the "late works are the catastrophe." They are that zone in which no unity is possible, in which all efforts at smoothing things out are defeated and the spikiness of lived experience must be encountered in unmitigated form. That word, "catastrophe": it makes us think immediately of the Nakba. Is Palestine, then, a form of lateness? That which is promised; that which must arrive; that which cannot but arrive; that which, nevertheless, is yet to arrive?

Ahed Tamimi spent more than half a year in an Israeli prison. She turned seventeen in prison. Why? For slapping a soldier the same day a soldier shot her cousin in the face. This asymmetry is intolerable, and should be intolerable. Thousands of Palestinians, many of them children, sit in Israeli jails because they rejected the insult to human dignity that is a military occupation. This is intolerable. It asks questions of all of us that demand answers. A dear friend of mine said, "As a German, I feel I should have no opinion on what Israel does." I can see what she is thinking, but I think she's badly mistaken. It is possible, and necessary, and essential, to be firmly opposed to anti-Semitism and to recognize, at the same time, the suffering of Palestinian people, and to do whatever must be done to bring that suffering to an end. There is no justice under the occupation.

3: BEIRUT

A couple of hours from Beirut, if you're fortunate with the traffic, you come within touching distance of the Syrian border. A course northward of that brings you through the Beqaa Valley and into Baalbek. We clambered through the palimpsest of ruins in Baalbek—the Assyrian, Roman, Byzantine, and Muslim ruins—and, wary of the proximity to the hot war just a few miles away, wondered if this is how people get kidnapped. That evening, coming back from the ruins, we thought we'd stop in Broummana, and see Edward Said's grave.

Literature is haunted by gravesite pilgrimages. The acolyte seeks blessings. But are these visits also apologies of a sort? Apologies for having been born too late? Every visit to a gravesite is an act of regret: for imperfect reading, for imperfect writing in the wake, for the unrepairable tear in the fabric of experience. But I was to have another regret, for our driver advised against a detour that night. It was late and he could not be sure of the roads. We returned to the city, and I never had the opportunity to go back. And yet, for the remainder of my time in Beirut, each time I passed by the building in Hamra that had been pointed out to me as the Said family home, I felt my heart race.

Late Beethoven emerges coherently out of mature Beethoven. Mature Beethoven is an extension and fulfillment of early Beethoven. These are major shifts and distinct modes of evolution that are nevertheless not radical breaks.

Said tells the story of meeting up with his friend Hanna Mikhail, whose nom de guerre was Abu Omar. This was in Beirut one night in 1972. Abu Omar had received his PhD in political theory at Harvard at the same time Said had gotten his in comparative literature there. In 1976, by that time long physically engaged in the struggle, and very much admired for his tremendous courage, Abu Omar disappeared with a number of others in a small boat in the waters off the Lebanese coast. No one ever knew what happened to them. But that earlier night in Beirut in 1972, as Said recounts it, Abu Omar showed up with none other than Jean Genet. The two men arrived at 10 p.m. The conversations lasted well into the night, until 3 a.m.

What a pang of recognition the story of Said, Jean Genet, and Abu Omar sparks in me. I am reminded of many late nights in Hamra with friends and recent acquaintances, over God knows how many bottles of arak. We discoursed late into the night—Marxists, Marxians, Greens, anarchists—with an intensity I have never seen matched elsewhere. I am talking of professors and graduate students and bar owners and autodidacts, all of whom seemed to have a powerful notion of how much was at stake, many of whom were younger than me, and all of whom had read much more than I had. The next morning, some would hurry away to go and read more and prepare themselves for the next night's discussion at one or another of the apartments we frequented, or at Mezyan, where everyone felt at home, and even the nonsmokers hung out outside so that nothing would be missed. And then there would be live bands, and the solitary walks home at 3 in the morning, in the safest nighttime streets I've ever known. I am so grateful for how relentless those engagements were, and the indefatigable energy of my companions, who made my three weeks in Beirut feel like three months.

At the heart of Op. 132 lies a slow movement which, in performance, can range from fifteen to close to twenty minutes. What matters is not the length but figuring out how to maintain and control the tension. The subtitle of that slow movement is: *Heiliger Dankgesang eines Genesenen an die Gottheit, in der lydischen Tonart*, "Hymn of Thanksgiving to God of an invalid on his convalescence, in the Lydian mode."

My Beirut friends were radical in the most beautiful sense. Said writes that "lateness . . . is a kind of self-imposed exile from what is generally acceptable, coming after it, and surviving beyond it." The old-fashioned political commitment and fearlessness I found in Beirut changed me. It was a kind of lateness, a kind of survival past the indifference that characterizes so much of American life. We thought about and talked about many things: what it meant to be both stateless and homeless, and what it meant to do right by those who were in that condition. We talked about how greed and profit drove human misery, and how pernicious remained the idea that certain races were superior to others.

The slow movement of Op. 132, with writing of stupendous and aching beauty, finally delivers what we had been seeking in the earlier movements: organic unity. Slow sections, of which there are three, all similar, alternate with fast sections. The slow sections of this middle movement are in two parts: an overlapping motif in the instruments and a profound and simple chorale. It is this chorale, with its intense light, that will never leave the listener, a light like that of T. S. Eliot's *Four Quartets*: "A glare that is blindness in the early afternoon. / And glow more intense than blaze of branch, or brazier . . ."

The fast sections are marked *Neue Kraft fühlend*, and are meant to suggest the feeling of strength coming back into the body. Again, Beethoven brings us into a realm of fluctuations. But the effect is very different here. Instead of the fever of the second movement, we now have two positive feelings: serenity alternating with vitality.

"Late" suggests two different ways of being off: to be before one's time is the more common, but to be after one's time, to be born too late, is equally poignant. When we consider the two in tandem, when we consider how Beethoven strikes us as inexpressibly old and also mysteriously well ahead of us, we come to the idea that he has somehow managed to elude time, that he is neither early nor late, that he is beyond time.

Near the end of the winding conversation between Farouq and Julius, Farouq gives an account of his stalled education at a Belgian university and the reason for his anger. He says: "I had applied to do an MA in Critical Theory because the department here was known for that. That was my dream, the way young people can have very precise dreams: I wanted to be the next Edward Said! And I was going to do it by studying comparative literature and using it as the basis for societal critique."

I think back to where my mind was when I wrote this passage. "I wanted to be the next Edward Said!" Where had that come from? I hadn't given the line to my difficult and occasionally unlikable narrator. I had given it to Farouq, a secondary character, a young man with whom I felt more sympathetic. So, was it that I wanted to be the next Edward Said myself? After all, in those years, in 2006 and 2007, I was in graduate school working on a PhD in art history, in the very university where Said had until recently been the star professor. But I don't think it was quite that simple. Writing fiction often contains an element of self-hypnosis, of flying in the dark. I already had intimations that the very book into which I was writing those words would be the book that led me out of academia. What I wanted to set down was the idea that Edward Said—what he wrote and who he was—was a kind of navigational help, an air traffic control tower for so many of us of so many different origins, talents, and ambitions. We were not supposed to become him, any more than he could have become the next Adorno or Benjamin. The ideal was to be in communication with his intuitions, and through them find our own way through the night.

In Beethoven's *Heiliger Dankgesang*, the use of the Lydian mode, an ancient mode, suggests something exotic, devotional, and mystically religious. Near the end of the movement is an instruction to play "with the most intimate emotions." In those final measures, you almost feel your soul rising out of you, separating itself from the body. The chorale builds and builds, and it is as though the prismatic colored lights you have been watching for a quarter of an hour merge of their own accord into a glare, into a blinding brightness, and then slowly dim in intensity. The effect is shattering.

4: BERLIN

The fourth and fifth movements of Op. 132 form a single unit, the one serving as a brief introduction to the other. The fourth movement is marked *Alla marcia*, "like a march," and this martial rhythm is interrupted again and again by a lighter playful section, rather like a father striding along in a serious manner while his daughter skips around him. Then comes a tremolo and recitative on the violin, a device reminiscent of the recitative that leads to the end of the composer's Ninth Symphony—"O Freunde!" In fact, the sketches for the end of Op. 132 were originally meant to provide an instrumental finale to Beethoven's Ninth, before he decided on a choral finale.

This bridging fourth movement is over in about two minutes, and we are suddenly in the fifth movement, *Allegro appassionato*, which begins elegantly, and has a yearning and passionate character. But there are elements that keep disrupting the meter, as previously happened in the second and fourth movements. The harried four outer movements of the quartet seem, in this sense, like jittery supplicants around the unassailable perfection of the *Heiliger Dankgesang*.

But here near the end of the quartet, the logic really does begin to build toward a unity. It is late Beethoven, but we note the classic Beethovenian arc of disparate elements assembling themselves out of struggle toward a harmonious conclusion. The cello, late in this fifth movement, cries out in a high and almost violinistic register. It is a startling effect, but the music is pulled back from the brink of terror, just in time, and the elegance that opens the movement returns. Many questions haunt late Beethoven, but it seems to me that one of the most persistent is: How does one make an ending?

My own lateness-haunted novel begins with late Mahler, *Das Lied von der Erde*, and ends with late Mahler, the Ninth Symphony, heard by my narrator in the final chapter of the novel in a performance by the Berlin Philharmonic. So the book physically ends in New York, but ends spiritually with an imagination of Berlin. When I first went to Berlin in 1999, I found it heavy with what I knew of its history. It was the dark core of the unspeakable. But Berlin is in some ways like a soul that came close to obliteration and, shocked by the experience, offers up a song of thanksgiving. I lived in the city in the summer of 2000 and, after that experience, found that the city began to evolve other meanings. I found myself returning. A week here, a month there, a sublime summer at the Literarisches Colloquium; the beloved museums, the late nights with irreplaceable friends, hip-hop and dancehall. Late Mahler, late Schoenberg, late Beethoven, and one never-to-be-forgotten afternoon at the Philharmonia, when Rattle conducted the Brahms Violin Concerto, and a friend flew over from Canada to witness it with me. And there was a special honor at the Haus der Kulturen der Welt, and my subsequent association with that organization. By degrees, Berlin became a city that taught me new things about the culture of memory.

Even deep in the strident march of the final *Allegro appassionato*, there are passages of intimate voice, a subtle chattering among the four instruments, like excitement heard from another room, or a part sung sotto voce. It is thought that it was this quartet specifically that inspired Eliot to write his own late, great *Four Quartets*. We certainly know that Eliot listened to Op. 132 again and again on the gramophone. And that he wrote to Stephen Spender, with typical Eliotian circumlocution, "I find it quite inexhaustible to study. There is a sort of heavenly or at least more than human gaiety about some of his later things which one imagines might come to oneself as the fruit of reconciliation and relief after immense suffering. I should like to get something of that into verse before I die." Perhaps he did:

With the drawing of this Love and the voice of this Calling
We shall not cease from exploration
And the end of all our exploring
Will be to arrive where we started
And know the place for the first time.

I love Edward Said's idea, drawn from his comparative study of literature, that difference is not about hierarchies but about the possibility of contrapuntal lines. Difference, at its best, interweaves and creates new harmonies. In a way, this was the positive argument put forth in *Orientalism*: a plea to reject stereotypes and to accept the irreducible complexity of the other. Understanding this, putting it into practical action, is the best hope for both our democracy and our ecology. Is it too much to say that we can love one another, and that we must? Counterpoint is also related to Said's concept of late style. Tension is sustained, stubbornness is unaccommodated, and difficulty is permitted. Lateness and newness live next to each other. The rest is music.

PART THREE

SHADOWS

Gossamer World:
On Santu Mofokeng

Out of a dark mass of inchoate forms, a single hand emerges and rests between two windows. There's an arm that places it there, and there is a dark sleeve around that arm. With closer looking, other hands and arms become apparent, some of them reaching for a rack above the windows. There are human bodies present, but only by implication. This is a scene of deep shadow and blur. The photographer is Santu Mofokeng, and the caption to the image opens up a world: "The Drumming, Johannesburg-Soweto Line, from Train Church, 1986" (figure 3). We now know that we are in South Africa, that the hand is not at rest, as we might first have guessed, but drumming on the wall of a train carriage, and that the train carriage is doing double duty as a church.

Mofokeng was born near Johannesburg in 1956. His photographs have a powerful, almost mesmerizing, effect on me. At least, now they do. When I first encountered them, many years ago, I didn't understand them. Something about them seemed unfinished, imprecise, or wrong. They looked like good ideas for photographs that never quite made it into actual good photographs. If ever I sought out a pictorial record of apartheid, classic

FIGURE 3. Santu Mofokeng, *The Drumming, Johannesburg-Soweto Line*, from *Train Church* (1986). Silverprint, © Santu Mofokeng Foundation. Photograph courtesy Lunetta Bartz, MAKER, Johannesburg.

photojournalism that lived up to the idea of the "decisive moment" seemed a better way to go. I could look at the work of the courageous and ingenious Ernest Cole, whose photographs proved valuable in the anti-apartheid struggle. Or, if I wanted images imbued with a quieter fury, I could turn to photographs by David Goldblatt, which showed, through photographs of people, landscapes, and buildings, both the infrastructure of South Africa and the lived experience of people under apartheid. Most of Goldblatt's photographs were well lit, in focus, and direct, with emotion kept to a minimum. I loved their form of witness. I still do.

My understanding of Mofokeng came more slowly. He grew up under apartheid, coming to a love for photography in his teens. He later found work as a darkroom assistant. In the mid-1980s, as a member of the photographers' collective Afrapix, he began to make images about daily life in the townships. Over a few weeks in 1986, during his commute to and from work, he made a series of remarkable photographs on the Soweto-Johannesburg train. Whether the ride was in the early morning, late afternoon, or evening, people congregated in the train's coaches, turning them into spaces of prayer and religious song. The train became a movable church.

His photographs captured the religious ecstasy of the commuters, their intense faces and dynamic bodies, just as any competent photographer would do. But Mofokeng did something else, or rather, something more: he made many of the photographs strange. The compositions are sometimes conventional, with clear figures and protagonists, but often they are dark, grainy, and blurry: a detail here and there, a hand, a jaw, a barely recognizable torso, areas of light flare. There are photographs only partly in focus and photographs not at all in focus; photographs that are all shadow and highlight, with little in the way of midtones. Several are off-kilter. You can viscerally feel the raucous atmosphere of the train church, the instability of the cabin, but also the mystery and consolation of religion. Mofokeng seems to test how many eccentricities a picture can tolerate before it breaks apart. He shoots in low light, nothing is ever quite level, figures seem to be where they are by chance, not "placed" as in more conventional pictures. There's too much foreground or too much background or simply a vast area where not a whole lot is happening. Like the conceptual artist John Baldessari, but without Baldessari's ironic tone, Mofokeng seems to embrace whatever makes a picture "wrong."

I came to understand that the use of open, seemingly fallow space as a compositional element was key to the power of Mofokeng's work. I look, for instance, at a photograph he made in 1989, on the occasion of the funeral of one Chief More, which took place near the village of GaMogopa. A gently undulating grassland dominates the scene. In the distance is a bus, in front of which is a hearse and a crowd of marchers. Behind the bus are two women, who might be walking intentionally slowly or trying to catch up with the main party. And in the foreground is a man, in whose body language we can definitively read a late-coming. He is hurrying to join the marchers, awkward in his isolation. Around them all is the great expanse of the landscape; the photo comes to feel less like an image of a funeral than an image of this space, in which the main event is almost too small to be properly seen. It is Mofokeng's ability to evoke a space like this one and its as-sociated slowness—an ability to permanently postpone any de-mand for a "main event" in the picture—that makes his work so distinctive.

• • •

"If your pictures aren't good enough, you're not close enough," Magnum cofounder Robert Capa once said (and has been for-ever quoted thereafter). But Mofokeng's pictures are often not "close enough," as at Chief More's funeral. Or they are too close, as in the train church photos. He locates the energy of the photo-graph elsewhere: in waiting, in uncertainty, in deep shadow. His photographs made the effects of oppression visible, but they were not primarily about that. He was drawn to the interstices of Afri-can life: worship services, concerts, funerals, civic activities, and the workaday world. The people in his photographs are kin to those the South African writer Alex La Guma evoked in his 1962 story "A Walk in the Night," people who hang around "idling, talk-ing, smoking, waiting." Mofokeng himself traveled long distances and would sometimes be stranded while working. He would go to townships, some of which he didn't know well, and hang around for days, allowing the sensibility of the place to enter his camera. I know of no photographer whose work contains so much of the drift that poorer folk know.

When Mofokeng left South Africa to study at the International Center of Photography in New York in 1991, through a scholarship named for Ernest Cole, he attended Roy DeCarava's workshops. It was a meeting of minds. The point is not that DeCarava was an influence (Mofokeng's voice was established before they met) but that both artists found productive use for stylistic reticence and literal obscurity. Perhaps no photographer since DeCarava has kept as much faith with shadows as Mofokeng has. Mofokeng's work did not seek to demystify the townships, just as DeCarava's did not seek to explain Harlem. The youths that Mofokeng captured in one photo from a 1988 concert in Sewefontein are extremely blurred, barely there. (And there's all the "extra" wall space to either side of them, which most photographers would avoid.) The most likely reason for the blur is that he was shooting at a low shutter speed, without a flash or a tripod. But the way the picture looks typifies another quality of his work, something Mofokeng has encapsulated through a word in his native Sesotho language: *seriti*. It is a word whose senses include "shadow" as well as "aura," "dignity," "presence," and "confidence." Against the harsh interrogative light of an unjust political reality, Mofokeng offers *seriti*: knowledge of a more secret sort.

Apartheid came to an end in South Africa in 1994, but the achievement of political freedom did not bring an end to Mofokeng's explorations. In fact they became more intense, because he saw that *seriti* was an undiminished aspect of Black South African life. And it is from this post-apartheid period that some of his most mysterious and boldly composed images arise. *Easter Sunday Church Service* (1996), for instance, from a series he called

Chasing Shadows, is dreamlike, full of smoke and scattered light, as devotees (most of them women in white head scarves) gather around for worship. Mofokeng took a keen interest particularly in church services that were held in the caves of Motouleng and Mautse, services that contained elements of traditional African religion. It was a situation in which reality and spirituality become inseparable. Mofokeng has written, of the atmosphere of these services, "While I feel reluctant to partake in this gossamer world, I can identify with it."

The spaciousness and blur of Mofokeng's pictures come ultimately from intimacy with this "gossamer world": a world that isn't insubstantial but that is elusive to the uninitiated, to outsiders. His photographs use a variety of techniques to adumbrate this world. The pictures drift away from picturesqueness and come closer to life itself, to *seriti*, and to the subtle range of associations embedded in that word. These are photographs of quiet disorder and imprecision, shadow-work and strategic refusal, evocations of what can neither be hurried along nor extinguished.

An Incantation for
Marie Cosindas

Marie Cosindas, who was born in Boston in September 1923 and
who died in the same city ninety-three years later, made photographs of such potency that they seem magical, dependent on
something beyond mere sleight of hand for their mesmerizing
effects and unified mood, so that the experience of looking at a
selection of them is like watching a single sentence unfurl over
several pages, driven along by an invisible inner consistency, not
unlike the atmosphere of imaginative abundance that Gabriel
García Márquez evoked in his novel *One Hundred Years of Solitude*, an atmosphere he used as the backdrop for the dense saga of
the Buendía family in the mythical town of Macondo, and especially in his account of the magician Melquíades, a "heavy Gypsy
with an untamed beard and sparrow hands," a bearer of dazzling
and arcane knowledge, including visions of the present and the
future, as well as the secrets of optics, telescopes, and magnetism,
so that many different kinds of insight seem to find a natural unity
inside him, and whose work reemerges in the final pages of the
novel in Sanskrit parchments, with "the even lines in the private
cipher of the Emperor Augustus and the odd ones in a Lace-

FIGURE 4. Marie Cosindas, *Memories II* (1976). Dye transfer print. © Estate of Marie Cosindas. Photograph courtesy Bruce Silverstein Gallery, New York.

daemonian military code," the inscrutabilities layered on one another to arrive at a startling lucidity of the kind that might be experienced by someone whose tangled dreams, regardless of their wildness or relentlessness, give way to a pure vision of wakefulness, though not the uninflected wakefulness of one who rises in early morning to a hot and innocent white light but rather the shadowed knowingness of one who has slept all day and awakes

to the infinitesimally graded colors of a deepening evening, a
moodiness recognizable to any viewer of Cosindas's photographs, which make the most of small, dark spaces, a talent that
perhaps originated in her being the eighth of ten children raised
by Greek immigrant parents in a small apartment in Boston's
South End, just as her experience as a child attending her parents'
Greek Orthodox church, with its gilded Byzantine icons and busy
walls, was possibly the origin of her luminous sense of color and
the suggestion of incense even when there is no smoke to be seen,
a dimension of her work which certainly did not arrive instanta-
neously, though it did finally arrive, after she had worked as a
painter and also as a photographer in black and white, including
time spent in the workshop of Ansel Adams, whose grayscale les-
sons she abandoned in order to take up color with an alchemical
force that is reminiscent of the great Amsterdam painter Rachel
Ruysch, a widely celebrated artist in the very first rank of still-life
painters of the Dutch golden age, who was active from the final
quarter of the seventeenth century until shortly before her death
in 1750 at age eighty-six, and who, moreover, was one of very few
women to be feted in that profession, and who outgrew both her
botanist father and painter husband, outshining them in reputation as she consolidated both botanical and artistic knowledge,
while raising ten children, to produce ferociously accurate bou-
quets of flowers, some of which were literal works of fiction that
showed in a single vase blooms that would have been seen in life
only in different seasons but which through the magical art of
painting could be permanently brought together, each precisely
painted and often accompanied by equally fine depictions of
marble plinths, tabletops, vases, and insects, the entire arrangement set against a dark background, as was the vogue during the
maturity of Dutch floral painting, a branch of art that saw the ele-

vation of the most modest and domestic material into an intensity that approached the sublime, a gift given to only a few: to leverage the ordinary into the glorious, to turn the soft petals of flowers into a flamelike radiance, much as Cosindas carefully selected subject matter and, through technical know-how and visual intelligence — a skillful deployment of lighting, filters, exposure times, developing times, and ambient temperature for florals but also other genres, including portraits and assemblages of objects of all kinds for which she disliked the term "still life," rightly rejecting any connotation of stasis, and for which she preferred "arrangement" — turned it into indelible statements about what photography could achieve more than half a century after pictorialism's heyday, with a use of color that was more soulful, by being somehow both freer and more disciplined, than what was generally seen in commercial color of the 1960s, and that came into the world earlier than the work of some other great color photography pioneers like William Eggleston, whose style was more deadpan, less arranged, less obviously artful, and more in keeping with the preference of critics and curators, once they acquired a taste for it, for what art photography in color should look like, though the louche and antiquarian work that Cosindas made did result in considerable fame for her in the '60s and '70s, with solo exhibitions at the Museum of Modern Art (before Eggleston), the Museum of Fine Arts, Boston, and the Art Institute of Chicago, but did not win her glory in most standard histories of photography, in which other artists, mostly younger than she and almost all male, are credited as the true pioneers of color, so that she came to be seen as an anomaly, neither modern nor contemporary, in part because her particular contribution to photography was mystical, sensuous, unashamed of beauty, and grounded in the combination of everyday objects with exotic ones, an earnestness that fit awkwardly with the ironic and occasionally cynical tastes that dominated the last half century but put her firmly in the line of many artists in history who were revolutionary not in founding a new school of thought but in discovering unexpected life in old approaches, not in keeping with the times but rather timeless, committing to the idea that magic is not a question of abandoning past knowledge but instead of marshaling a vast trove of elements into a hypnotic flow, which in Cosindas's case meant the discovery of the emotional impact that could result from making dye-diffusion transfer prints with a view camera and the way that, over time, a world of props, references, and cues could be constructed into a singular artistic voice, an ensorcelled world that included flowers, vases, dolls, lace, fur, rugs, porcelain, books, chairs, oranges, asparagus, posters, ornaments, statues, dancers, dandies, sailors, tarot cards, masks, and puppets, but also those portals into other worlds—paintings, mirrors, and windows—that collectively constituted a highly personal vision of reality enamored of theatrical effects and attuned to the inner life of inanimate things, to the animism they harbor, a receptivity rather like that of Rainer Maria Rilke's narrator in *The Notebooks of Malte Laurids Brigge*, a young boy in Denmark who discovers wardrobes in which generations of costumes are kept, and who, trying them on, begins to experience their uncanny transformational power, so that even as he looks at himself in the mirror, arrayed in these strange clothes, the mirror seems to him to not quite believe its eyes, such that, to the boy, what is there is now "something very astonishing, strange, totally different" from what he had imagined, "something sudden, independent," an experience that only intensifies with further episodes of dressing up until one day he disguises himself so thoroughly that he spooks himself and flees screaming from the mirror, though it should be said that a connection between the alchemy in Cosindas's photographs and the weirdness registered by other artists is not a simple question of influence or imitation, or even a claim that magic of this kind always works in the same way, but rather that there are often similar intuitions between practitioners in this shamanic mode, all of whose work seems to be a bewitching murmur, always placid but glimmering with the possibility of ensnaring the viewer, a paradox that is true of Cosindas's densely woven pictures, the assemblages that she spent days putting together and that evoke spaces redolent of complexity like the kitchens of great cooks or the laboratories of ancient perfumers, spaces in which unexplained things happen, exemplified in her *Floral with Marie Cosindas Painting, Boston* (1965), *Masks, Boston* (1966), and *Memories II* (1976; figure 4), grand dreams faintly fringed by nightmare, so that you no longer think only of "Marie Cosindas," the photographer, but of "the Great Cosindas," a Melquíades-like Magus whose photographs put you under a spell with their dashes of color and pointillist passages, their areas of deep shadow and hints at secret meaning, their winelike darkness, robust, intoxicating, and dangerous, their quiet watchfulness and brooding air of enchantment, their perfect stillness and readiness to pounce, like mirrors so full of life that you could plunge right into them and only with great difficulty find a way out.

Pictures in the Aftermath

In an essay titled "Late-Night Thoughts on Listening to Mahler's Ninth Symphony," the physician and essayist Lewis Thomas wrote, "I cannot listen to the last movement of the Mahler Ninth without the door-smashing intrusion of a huge new thought: death everywhere, the dying of everything, the end of humanity." Thomas was talking about the likelihood of nuclear apocalypse. The essay was published in his 1983 book of the same title. When I first read it in the mid-1990s, I appreciated its mournful lyricism, even as I encountered it as a time capsule of the worries of a different generation.

I've been thinking of Thomas's essay again. Some video clips of American nuclear-weapons tests from the 1950s and '60s were recently made available to the public for the first time, and a few dozen of them were uploaded to YouTube by the Lawrence Livermore National Laboratory. Many are shorter than a minute, and none are longer than eight minutes. On the flickering screen, I have been watching various iterations of the infamous nuclear cloud spraying radioactivity into the atmosphere above Nevada or the Pacific. Several of the clips simply show a mysterious white circle glowing against a dark field. We can watch these videos because they have now been declassified, assessed as belonging safely to the past. But the fears Thomas wrote about back in the '80s now feel real to me. The nation's nuclear stance is back to belligerence, one more significant turn for the worse in a world suddenly full of turns for the worse. Considered with one eye on current news, the clips are terrifying and mesmerizing, and are made more so by the absence of sound. The unspeakable unfolds in silence.

If Americans are back to brooding about nuclear disaster, Japanese people have had no break from it since the Second World War. There was the staggering legacy of being the only nation to have been attacked with nuclear weapons, the two American bombs that destroyed Hiroshima and Nagasaki. This legacy permeates Japanese society at all levels, provoking questions about what it means to mourn, to move on, or to confront the past as both aggressor and victim.

Japan's subsequent embrace of nuclear-power plants was a fateful choice in a country not only laden with such a traumatic past but also vulnerable to earthquakes and tsunamis. The earthquake that struck in the Pacific off the coast of Tohoku, in the northeastern part of Honshu, in March 2011 triggered an enormous tsunami that caused immense damage: towns were flooded, infrastructure was wrecked, forests were splintered, and more than fifteen thousand people died. The earthquake cut off the external power supply to the Daiichi nuclear power plant in Fukushima, and floodwaters from the tsunami damaged the plant's backup generators and disabled its cooling system. Overheating ensued. Fuel in three of the reactor cores melted, leading to a release of radiation. And so to the fast-moving disaster of a tsunami was added the slow-motion disaster of a nuclear calamity.

The tripartite catastrophe of earthquake, tsunami, and nuclear accident is known in Japan as 3/11, because it began on March 11. The calendrical naming indicates something of the seriousness with which those events were viewed. And as befits a date so crucial, there has been a varied and widespread set of responses to it — in politics, of course, but also in journalism, photography, literature, and in the arts in general. The 3/11 disaster was perhaps the first major one in Japan to be so thoroughly captured as it unfolded. Footage from surveillance cameras and webcams shows the water coming in, the roads being swept away and the towns and harbors being destroyed. And in the immediate aftermath, extensive documentary work was undertaken by photographers from Japan and abroad. The meticulous photographic documentation of ruins, debris, cleanup, and relief operations by the photojournalist Kazuma Obara was typical: his pictures showed the gut-wrenching scale of the destruction, the professionalism of the emergency crews, and the fortitude of the survivors.

But with the passage of time, less direct photographic responses to 3/11 began to emerge, and many of Japan's most respected photographers turned their attentions to Tohoku. Shortly after the earthquake, the Japanese government put into effect a zone of exclusion around the damaged Fukushima power plant that forbade unauthorized persons to breach an invisible perimeter at a radius of twenty kilometers from the reactors (a semicircle on land, because the other half of the circle was in the Pacific Ocean).

The photographer Tomoki Imai undertook a two-year project of photographing the irradiated landscape. The photographs in his series *Semicircle Law* were made at different locations on or near the twenty-kilometer perimeter, with his large-format camera directed at the damaged reactors in the distance. Sometimes the reactors are barely visible, and often they aren't visible at all. The resulting images are simple landscapes in various seasons. Some of them are banal; others are beautifully pensive. They are decisively transfigured only by our knowledge of the circumstances under which they were made.

Equally subtle is the work of Shimpei Takeda, which at first glance looks like a series of images of the night sky. But his white-flecked black pictures are actually photographs of the soil—or, more accurately, they are photograms, as they were made without a camera. Takeda obtained soil samples from a number of locations around Fukushima and nearby prefectures and placed them on photosensitive film in a light-tight chamber for a month. Depending on the amount of radioactivity in the soil, the film may register a few dots, white when printed, or enough to create nebula-like white splotches. These enigmatic images make visible the otherwise unseen toxicity of the ground.

I saw Imai's and Takeda's images in 2017 at an exhibition of post–World War II Japanese photography at the San Francisco Museum of Modern Art. In the same exhibition was work by Rinko Kawauchi, whose ability to infuse gentle diaristic images with intense spiritual power I have long admired. Kawauchi's response to 3/11 (not presented in the San Francisco exhibition) was published in a book titled *Light and Shadow*. A key theme of her sequence of photographs was a pair of pigeons, one black, the other white. Kawauchi photographed them in and above the wreckage of Tohoku, often capturing them both in a single frame. In Kawauchi's account, these birds were homing pigeons rendered distraught by the devastation below, circling restlessly, uncertain where to land. Their starkly oppositional colors lent the series a further air of symbolism and a sense of the miraculous.

We make images in response to disaster. Seeing is part of our coming to terms. Oblique responses, like those by Imai, Takeda, and Kawauchi to 3/11, are especially resonant because they are reactions to a tragedy, but they also reach beyond it and give us new language. A focused and delimited view of the catastrophe is offered, and this delimitation enables the images to transcend their subject.

As I silently watch the grim old footage of American bomb tests, it occurs to me that the unsteady black-and-white imagery, decontextualized, begins to hint at abstraction. Like the photographs from Japan, it is simultaneously primordial and futuristic. The extreme uncertainty I feel in our current political moment helps me understand for the first time the curious twinship of mourning and premonition. What was endured can hint at what is yet to come. Takeda's radioactive cosmos, Imai's brooding landscapes, and Kawauchi's dazed pigeons take me through several registers of thought simultaneously: information about the tragedy, sorrow for the suffering it caused, gratitude for the work that makes that sorrow visible, foreboding about the future.

On any given day, an alert might flash across your phone. Something terrible has happened far away, a flood, an airstrike. Soon, there's footage of people picking through the wreckage of what used to be their homes. It is easy to pity them, but difficult to imagine that this could be you, that you are the one suddenly bereft of a solid place in the world. And yet it is precisely this expectation of solidity, this notion that things are probably going to be fine, that I sense falling away from us once again. Listening now to Mahler's Ninth Symphony, I find it inflected by Lewis Thomas's essay, and steeped in a gloom similar to his. It's not just Mahler's Ninth that brings up these feelings: listening to anything that touches on the sublime makes me apprehensive, whether it's Coltrane, Björk, or even the loaded silence that greets me when I wake up in the middle of the night.

I think of the reckless policies being rushed into law all around us, the undermining of scientific consensus, the breakdown of diplomacy, the tweeting president and his confrontational temperament, and I wonder which events we in America are doomed to undergo in our own turn, events we may already be well in the middle of, whether by an act of war or by an act of God, whether with a nuclear element or not, events that will expose our utter unreadiness, alter our experience of the world permanently and require us to find new ways of seeing, and new ways of mourning.

Shattered Glass

After mass killings, American newspapers do not typically run images of corpses. The reasons have to do with respect for the dead and concern for readers' sensitivities, as well as restrictions put on photojournalists' access to crime scenes (these conventions are subtly, and unjustly, different when it comes to international stories). Instead of photographs of bloody bodies in the street, we get photographs of ambulances, medical and law enforcement professionals, people ducking for cover. One photograph we've all seen shows someone in distress being cradled in someone else's arms. Another records the candlelit vigils held in the aftermath of these horrors. The raw pathos inherent in such moments is now dulled; seen once too often, the situations are not as moving as they ought to be. But even with these diminishing returns, the press is obligated to run pictures. Among them, which are piercing? Which endure? The minor ones, the odd and peculiar ones, the ones that evoke some other history.

The images that have stayed with me from the 2017 Las Vegas massacre are of broken glass. Stephen Paddock sprayed bullets down on country-music concertgoers from a suite on the thirty-second floor of the Mandalay Bay resort, smashing two of its windows in order to do so. He killed at least fifty-eight people, and injured hundreds more. For photographers arriving after the massacre, it would have made sense to look up and shoot the building (the shared vocabulary between cameras and firearms is both regrettable and illuminating), aiming in the direction opposite that of the killer's nighttime shots. What these photographers would have seen was a golden building, its front part protuberant and vaguely ship-shaped. The hotel's windows are gaudy in the Vegas style, covered with a thin film of gold. Near the top of the building are two irregular shapes, nine panels apart, one near the front of the building's prow, the other further to starboard. They look like small black stains or asterisks, or perhaps even a pair of gouged-out eyes: these are the broken windows.

The post-massacre photographs of the building are documents of fact. They do not feel like "works of art," nor are they intended to be. But they have a collective ability to draw our attention to the void behind the broken windows, not only the unilluminated void where windows were broken, but also the inhumane void that possessed the murderer's soul, the mournful void that overtook the survivors, and the abysmal void beneath our way of life, from which a bewildering violence erupts incessantly.

Glass is everywhere in photography. From Eugène Atget's reflective vitrines to Lee Friedlander's sly self-portraiture, photographers have long been in thrall to the visual complications glass can inject into a composition. Glass is present not only as photography's seductive subject but also as its physical material. In the nineteenth century, photographs were commonly made on wet-plate negatives, glass coated with photosensitive emulsion, and then on the improved and portable dry-plate negatives, before, in the twentieth century, film was manufactured with sufficient

FIGURE 5. André Kertész, *Broken Plate, Paris* (negative 1929; print 1970s). Gelatin silver print. © Estate of André Kertész. Photograph: higherpictures.

strength to serve as a transportable base for the emulsion. Sometimes the very glass of the negative becomes part of the photograph's story.

André Kertész photographed a view over Montmartre in 1929, presumably through an open window. He left Paris and moved to New York and was not reunited with the negative until the 1960s, by which time it was cracked and badly damaged (figure 5). But this damage became the story. Looking at Kertész's 1970 print of the negative, it's easy to think that what we are seeing is a photograph of a city through a broken window, perhaps one shot through with a bullet. It is in fact a photograph of a city printed from a damaged glass-plate negative.

Broken glass, and broken windows in particular, are a notable byway in photography's history. Brett Weston made one of the most striking examples in San Francisco in 1937. Weston was not recording evidence of a crime, or even particularly making a sociological comment. He was describing an abstraction with his camera, the calligraphic presence of a jagged black hole surrounded by a gray remnant of glass. What has been broken away dominates the picture. We see an outline like a map of a fictional island. There's more dark to see here than glass, and the darkness is deep and mysterious, a mouth agape in an unending scream. John Szarkowski, the influential curator at the Museum of Modern Art, wrote that this black shape "is not a void but a presence; the periphery of the picture is background." In the middle, in that darkness, is where Weston's self-portrait would be, if the window were intact.

Brett Weston was the son of the great photographer Edward Weston, and he shared his father's attraction to the mesmerizing abstractions that everyday objects can harbor. But the younger Weston's unique talent was to balance finely, over a long career, the competing demands of something and nothing, not simply of shape but also of the absence of shape, and to create strongly graphic pictures out of those tensions. He returned to the subject of broken windows more than once, but even in his other pictures — like one of Mendenhall Glacier, made in 1973 and printed in high contrast, or one of peeling paint on a Portuguese wall, from 1971, the paint dark and the wall beneath pale — he seemed to be pursuing the same highly contrasted, strongly gestural concerns.

The avant-garde German photographer Ilse Bing's broken window in Paris, from 1934, is crisp and cutting like Weston's — but we've taken several steps back, and we see a substantial part of a building's facade, including another window. It is now therefore a picture with context, and that context is poverty. Aaron Siskind's repeated studies of broken windows zoom farther in, excluding most of the frames and leaving us with abstract-expressionist patterns that give as much space to glass as to its absence. Brassaï and Gordon Matta-Clark have pictures that delight in a series of broken windows, serried ranks of angular splotches, like verse after verse of a ragged song. Paolo Pellegrin's *A Gypsy Woman on the Train*, made in Kosovo in 2001, is as much about the apprehensive passenger's face as it is about the damaged window next to her; together they evoke war and displacement. But these photographs all have something in common. Every broken window is a frozen shock.

Among the broken-window photographs of the Mandalay Bay resort, there are intriguing variants. In some, a spectator can be seen at ground level, behind a strip of police tape. Some photographers took advantage of the proximity of the Las Vegas airport to the Las Vegas Strip, making images that juxtapose the resort with Air Force One, which brought the president on a visit three days after the massacre. One such photo shows the plane at the airport with the golden structure in the distance behind. Another, by the Reuters photographer Mike Blake, shows Air Force One flying past the building. It manages to present the glory of airplane technology and the fragility of glass in a single image (and brings to mind a photo of the Graf Zeppelin printed from a cracked dry-plate glass negative in 1929: flight and broken glass together). Blake's photo places the scene of the crime side by side with the presidential plane: it's almost a political statement. But a statement saying what? That the president is ignoring the problem? That his presence is a consolation to a frightened nation? It is a clear picture, but it has no clear political meaning.

Many of our encounters with photographs today, whether

taken by us or made by others, are through the glass of a mobile phone. The mobile phone is a kind of window, and it is always on the verge of breaking. The image world, echoing the real world, is correspondingly fragmentary. This is perhaps what makes the various photographs of the broken windows at the Mandalay Bay resort so poignant. And perhaps, here, we do have a political lesson. An intact window is interesting mainly for its transparency. But when the window breaks, what intrigues us is the brittleness that was there all along.

PLATE 1. Caravaggio, *The Beheading of Saint John the Baptist* (1608). Oil on canvas. St. John's Co-Cathedral, Valleta. Photograph: Wikimedia.

PLATE 2. Caravaggio, *The Raising of Lazarus* (1609). Oil on canvas. Museo Regionale, Messina. Photograph: Wikimedia.

PLATE 3. Susan Meiselas, *Neighbors watch as dead bodies are burned in the streets* (1979). Esteli, Nicaragua. Photograph © Susan Meiselas/Magnum Photos.

PLATE 4. Kerry James Marshall, *Untitled (Underpainting)* (2018). © Kerry James Marshall. Acrylic and collage on PVC. Photograph: David Zwirner Gallery, London.

PLATE 5. Lorna Simpson, *Montage* (2018). Ink and acrylic on gessoed wood. Five panels, each 170.2 × 127 × 3.5 cm (67 × 50 × 1⅜ in.); overall, 170.2 × 635 × 3.5 cm (67 × 250 × 1⅜ in.). Unique. © Lorna Simpson. Courtesy of the artist and Hauser & Wirth. Photograph: James Wang.

PLATE 6. Yoruba (Ife) artist, Obalufon mask (12th century?). Copper. Height, 29.5 cm (11⅝ in.). National Museum, Lagos. From *Art and Life in Africa* (https://africa.uima .uiowa.edu; NML014). Photograph: Dirk Bakker.

PLATE 7. Duccio di Buoninsegna, *The Raising of Lazarus* (1310–1311). Tempera and gold on panel. Kimbell Art Museum, Fort Worth. Photograph: Wikimedia.

PLATE 8. Teju Cole, *Oslo* (2018).

What Does It Mean
to Look at This?

A photograph of a group of suffering people: we look at them, and from the sadness of their expressions and gestures, we know something awful has happened. But finding out exact details, through the photograph alone, is more difficult. Who these sufferers are, why they suffer, who or what caused the suffering, and what ought to be done about it—these are altogether more complex questions, questions hard to answer by only looking at the photograph.

The accounts journalists typically give of their motivations, particularly for photographing violence, aren't always convincing. Why go off to wars or conflict zones at great personal risk to take pictures of people whose lives are in terrifying states of disarray? The answer is often tautological: the images are physically dangerous and psychologically costly to make, and therefore they must be the right images. Susan Sontag, probably the most influential writer on the intersection of violence and photography, didn't buy this argument. With forensic prose, she cut through complacent apologias for war photography and set photojournalistic images of violence squarely in the context of viewers' voyeurism. This was the argument advanced in her 1977 essay collection, *On Photography*. Sontag believed that a certain passivity was inescapable in spectatorship, and that any image of violence would be tainted by this passive distance. "Through the camera people become customers or tourists of reality," she wrote. Looking at images of violence, she seemed to suggest, was both self-absorbed and self-absolving.

She revisited the subject near the end of her life, with more complexity. In *Regarding the Pain of Others* (2003), she still viewed photojournalists with skepticism (she dubbed them "star witnesses" and "specialized tourists"), and remained averse to the kind of prurient gaze that images of torment can foster. But she amended some of her earlier positions. She had previously argued that photographs, despite their capacity to generate sympathy, could quickly shrivel it through overexposure. She became less sure about that. She also queried the idea, implicit in her earlier arguments and explicit in the work of theorists like Guy Debord and Jean Baudrillard, that the abundance and distribution of images made reality itself little more than a spectacle:

> It suggests, perversely, unseriously, that there is no real suffering in the world. But it is absurd to identify the world with those zones in the well-off countries where people have the dubious privilege of being spectators, or of declining to be spectators, of other people's pain, just as it is absurd to generalize about the ability to respond to the sufferings of others on the basis of the mind-set of those consumers of news who know nothing at first hand about war and massive injustice and terror.

Sontag wondered, near the end of *Regarding the Pain of Others*, whether "one has no right to experience the suffering of others at a distance, denuded of its raw power," and she came to the conclusion that sometimes a bit of distance can be good. "There's nothing wrong with standing back and thinking," she wrote. (Even more than the incisiveness of her judgments, Sontag's willingness to reconsider her previous views is what endears her to me.)

The challenges of viewership have only intensified in the twenty-first century. Images of violence have both proliferated and mutated, demanding new forms of image literacy. Some recent scholars of photography have argued with some of Sontag's assertions in *On Photography*. One of those scholars, Ariella Azoulay, has questioned the claim of voyeurism. Azoulay reads images of conflict or atrocity as constituting a more interwoven set of actors, displacing the question from one of voyeurism, or even of empathy, to one of participatory citizenship. We are all in this together, Azoulay seems to be saying (and I don't think the Sontag of *Regarding the Pain of Others* would disagree). In making such an argument, Azoulay attends to a different tradition of writing about photography, one connected to an assertion made in 1857 by Lady Elizabeth Eastlake in the *London Quarterly Review*: "For it is one of the pleasant characteristics of this pursuit that it unites men of the most diverse lives, habits and stations, so that whoever enters its ranks finds himself in a kind of republic, where it needs apparently but to be a photographer to be a brother."

But in Azoulay's view, it is not only being a photographer that grants a person admission to this imaginative republic. Being the subject of photos, no less than taking photos or looking at photos, is one of a set of mutually reinforcing activities in which the participants are interdependent and complicit. The meaning of any given image arises from these various roles as well as that of the camera itself. This is one of the points Azoulay makes at length in her lucid and indispensable 2008 study, *The Civil Contract of*

Photography. Her argument rests on the civic relations between people: "When and where the subject of the photograph is a person who has suffered some form of injury, a viewing of the photograph that reconstructs the photographic situation and allows a reading of the injury inflicted on others becomes a civic skill, not an exercise in aesthetic appreciation." Azoulay's project arose out of her own experiences as a Jewish Israeli citizen who, nevertheless, had to interpret the images she was seeing of Palestinian suffering. Are these people radically other, or are they somehow included in the general "we"?

. . .

Photographs of atrocity always confront us with questions of inequality. But these questions can no longer simply be reduced to "Why them and why not us?" If, as Azoulay argues, photography deterritorializes citizenship, then these images accuse, they interrogate, and they put us in the same boat with those we are looking at. "What have we done," they ask us, "to create the conditions in which others, our fellow citizens, undergo these unspeakable experiences?"

The scholar Susie Linfield critiques Sontag in different terms. In *The Cruel Radiance* (2010), Linfield defends what she sees as the noble ideals of documentary photography. She finds fault with a number of notable photography critics (Sontag, as well as Roland Barthes and John Berger, among others) for being distrustful of photography, for not loving it enough. Sontag is, to Linfield, a "brilliant skeptic," and Linfield finds this a much less attractive persona than the one of the "smitten lover," which is what she deems the film critic Pauline Kael. What photography can do especially well, in Linfield's view, is present the ways in which the ideals of human rights fall short. A photograph cannot show human rights, but it can depict, with terrifying realism, what a starving person looks like, what a human body looks like after it has been shot. "Photographs show how easily we are reduced to the merely physical, which is to say how easily the body can be maimed, starved, splintered, beaten, burnt, torn and crushed."

This is sharply observed. But the devil is in the details, and the kind of details photographs are good at are visual and affective, different from the kind of details we might call "political," which have to do with laws, shades of linguistic meaning, and the distribution of power. For all her optimism about the efficacy of photography, Linfield admits that "we, the viewers, must look outside the frame to understand the complex realities out of which these photographs grew."

In *Regarding the Pain of Others*, Sontag wrote, "The photographer's intentions do not determine the meaning of the photograph, which will have its own career, blown by the whims and loyalties of the diverse communities that have use for it." The truth of the statement is obvious in certain cases, such as that of the notorious photographs made in late 2003 by Private Charles Graner Jr. and others at the Abu Ghraib prison in Iraq. In stripping prisoners naked, piling them up into a pyramid, or ordering them to masturbate, Private Graner and other American soldiers might have intended to use humiliation to "soften" their prisoners up for interrogation. But the images, once they were released into the world, had a much more shocking and enraging meaning.

Or consider the case of the Syrian photographer code-named Caesar. He was making photographs, with a team, as part of his military-police job. Disturbed at the increasing number of gruesome murders he had to photograph, he began to smuggle out large numbers of images — images of thousands of people starved, beaten, or tortured to death by the Syrian state — between the fall of 2011 and the summer of 2013. Caesar himself eventually escaped Syria. His images, initially made for one purpose (as the regime's records of its enemies), came to take on a different significance (as evidence of astonishing crimes against humanity). The gap between the photographer's intention and the subsequent life of the image is usually not as significant as in these two cases. But there's always some kind of disjuncture, a disjuncture that arises from photography's tendency to show only so much but often to mean much more: a photograph's tendency, in other words, to connote more than it denotes. As Tina Campt has written, photographs don't speak, but they are not mute. They are quiet, and solicit a kind of listening.

. . .

A photograph of a group of suffering people: it registers at first as a familiar type of image, the expertly made photograph of an atrocity in a faraway country (plate 3). The photographer's expertise expresses itself through color and visual rhythm; despite the subject matter, it is a beautiful photograph. We see five people: four women and one man. They are surrounded by rubble. On a blue door or wall is graffiti. The man and three of the women have clapped their hands to their mouths and noses, or raised their hands to cover their faces, as though they are simultaneously grieving and protecting themselves from a stench. The fourth woman has averted her eyes. Something horrible is going on, something we can't see.

But what does the photograph, by itself, tell us about what that "something" is? Not much. Unless it is supported with extra-photographic evidence, it will be limited to platitudes about human brutality or the universality of grief, truths for which no photographic argument is required. At the most basic level, that extra evidence begins with the caption: "Susan Meiselas. Neighbors watch as dead bodies are burned in the streets of Estelí, 1979." The caption gives us the photographer's name, establishes a place and time, and also gives us a plain description of an event. But if we stop there, we have only decorated the image with a bit of knowledge. Further investigation might reveal that Estelí is a city in northern Nicaragua, and that in early 1979, a popular struggle by the Sandinistas to unseat the dictator Anastasio Somoza Debayle was gaining strength. We might discover that the dead bodies just out of sight in Meiselas's picture were of people killed by Somoza's National Guard. The people in the photograph were reacting, Meiselas said, to "the intensity of putrefied bodies that have been on the street for three to five days in the hot sun." Out there photographing, she could smell them. We almost can, too.

This single photograph could be supported by a shelf's worth of books: about the history of Nicaragua, about right-wing regimes, about Latin America in the late '70s, about leftist dreams of revolution, about American foreign policy, about the sense of smell, about the personal courage of a woman photographing in a war zone, about the political economy of Estelí, and so on. The photograph cannot do that all by itself, but it can occasion those investigations.

Recognizing the frustration of trying to make photographs speak to the incredible complexity of civil conflict, Meiselas has written, of her time in Nicaragua, "I had photographs, they have a revolution." In the course of 1978 and 1979, she made hundreds of photographs. She made many more in subsequent visits. What difference did those photographs make? Moreover, what could be more irritating, and even offensive, than to have someone photographing you while you mourn the burning of a relative's body? Would you want a photographer there, clicking away, on the worst day of your life?

I return to Azoulay's idea that the photograph functions as a bond between the photographer and the photographed, that it's a kind of promise made by the first of these people to the second: *I will bear witness to this.* In their grief, in their shock, even in their irritation at the presence of a photographer, the hope for those who are photographed in the midst of their suffering is that what is happening to them will go out into the world, and possibly, by being seen, will help bring them relief.

Proof of this is elusive. We've all seen war photographs that are mere grist for the journalistic mill. Some photographers *are* addicted to war, and some viewers *are* voyeurs; and yet photography is not limited by these ways of seeing. Photography works and doesn't work, it is tolerable and intolerable, it confounds and often exceeds our expectations. "Conflict photography," in particular, arises out of a huge set of moving variables that in unpredictable, unreliable, but unignorable ways help make the demands of justice visible. Taking photographs is sometimes a terrible thing to do, but often, not taking the necessary photo, not bearing witness, or not being allowed to do so can be worse.

A Crime Scene at the Border

On Tuesday, June 25, 2019, Rosa Ramírez was filmed at home in San Martín, El Salvador. Ramírez stands by a doorway in a small interior. She is distraught, and her large brown eyes glisten in the glare of camera lights. "The last message he sent me was Saturday. He said, 'Mama, I love you.' He said, 'Take care of yourselves because we are fine here.'"

Her face is puffy from weeping.

"When I read that message, I don't know, it made me want to cry because I saw it as a sort of goodbye."

· · ·

The man lies face down in water, his black shirt more than halfway hiked up his back. A toddler, also face down, is tangled up in his shirt. They lie side by side, her arm draped across his neck. He wears black shorts. She wears red pants pulled up past the calves, tiny shoes, and we see the telltale bulge of a diaper. Blue beer cans bob in gray-green water around them. The rushes on the riverbank grow profusely. The photo shows Rosa Ramírez's son, Óscar

Alberto Martínez Ramírez, and his daughter, Valeria, and it was taken by the Mexican photojournalist Julia Le Duc.

Oscar Martínez and Valeria had traveled from El Salvador and had been in Mexico a couple of months. Disheartened by a torturous asylum process, they tried to swim across the Rio Grande from Matamoros to Brownsville, Texas. That is where they both drowned. Martínez was twenty-five, Valeria nearly two. In the video made three days later, Rosa Ramírez speaks as one for whom all hope is gone. The previous Saturday, she was reading a message from her son. By Tuesday, with the cameramen recording, she had herself become news.

Martínez and Valeria are two of the hundreds of people who will die on the United States–Mexico border before the year 2019 is through. They are two of the thousands who have died in the past decade in awful circumstances. On the border, people have died alone or with others, in the desert or in water, of exhaustion or of thirst, or shot with bullets, their bodies left to the elements or wild animals.

. . .

When the Associated Press distributed Le Duc's photograph around the world, it did so within the conventions of news reporting: something happened somewhere, someone photographed it, the image was picked up by a news agency, and it went out to the international press. The photograph was published in the pages of the *New York Times*, the *Washington Post*, the *Guardian*, the *Wall Street Journal*, and countless others. In news reports and opinion columns, it was lauded as an act of witness, and the hope was widely expressed that it might activate the conscience of the American government and spur a change on the border.

Brutal images easily elicit sympathy. It is true that a very few images of suffering have catalyzed changes in policy, but it is equally true that terrible images are published all the time, thousands of them each year, and the vast majority change policy not one iota. There have been truly astonishing, and truly sickening, photos from Gaza, Lampedusa, Yemen, Kashmir. But governments, in spite of an abundance of memorable photographs, regularly fail to honor the legitimate claims made before them by persons seeking safety and dignity.

Perhaps too much is made of individual photographs. What if we had, for each incident, not one photograph, but a hundred? What if we had photographs taken across the span of time showing not just what happened in Matamoros in June 2019 but what led to it? Would we be able to hold on to our innocence?

. . .

In the 1980s, Presidents Ronald Reagan and George H. W. Bush supported El Salvador's military-led government in a civil war against various leftist groups. The government's atrocities have been well documented, and tens of thousands of Salvadorans died. Hundreds of thousands more fled to the United States. In the mid-1990s, President Bill Clinton allowed the "temporary protected status" of Salvadoran refugees to expire after the end of the civil war there, and many of those who were forced to go back formed or joined the gangs at the core of the current violence in that country. In June 2014, President Barack Obama boasted that Border Patrol agents "already apprehend and deport hundreds of thousands of undocumented immigrants every year." In 2017, dozens of suspected gang members were illegally executed by United States–funded Salvadoran security forces.

In January 2018, the White House announced its intention to end temporary protected status for nearly two hundred thousand people who had come to the United States from El Salvador after a series of devastating earthquakes there in 2001. The effect of this would be to cut off the ability of those people to support poor relatives back home, threatening further injury to an already wounded Salvadoran economy. In April of the same year, Border Patrol agents began implementing a "metering" policy that slowed the processing of asylum claims at the United States–Mexico border to a trickle, creating a huge backlog. In June 2019, the United States vowed to provide no further aid to Guatemala, Honduras, and El Salvador until they reduced the migration of their nationals to the United States—a cruel and counterproductive measure.

How would such a relentless catalog of inhumane policy be photographed? Momentous political decisions, often made by men in suits in quiet, evenly lit rooms, do not tend to generate visual drama. The photographs might only show someone signing a document or someone in the middle of a speech. They might show a president, a member of Congress, a Border Patrol agent, a lobbyist, a judge, a citizen at a political rally or in a voting booth.

What if these photographs, in all their bureaucratic banality, were presented alongside the photograph of two drowned people? It would be a strange juxtaposition, a strangeness out of which some vital truth might be articulated. And what if the photograph with the dead bodies was omitted entirely and only the policies that led to the deaths were shown? Would we still be shocked and saddened? Or do we always need the spectacle of corpses to make the story real?

. . .

The media's defense of the publication of Le Duc's photograph was familiar: that it is the job of the press to disseminate the truth, no matter how bitter, and that by showing the bitterest truth, some justice might be done. But a photograph of a dead child on the United States–Mexico border is not, by itself, the bitterest truth. A bitterer truth might be to convey that what we are looking at is a crime, not an accident. The bitterest truth might be to show that the crime was committed by the viewers of the photograph, that this is not news from some remote and unconnected reality but, rather, something you have done, not you personally but you as a member of the larger collective. It is *you* who have undermined their democracy, *you* who have devastated their economy, *you* who have denied their claim to asylum. These are not strangers requesting a favor. They are people you already know, confronting you with your misdeeds.

That is not how such images are typically presented or understood. So, what happens if evidence of your crimes is presented to you over and over again but you do not accept culpability? What happens is that your assessment of the evidence becomes ever more disingenuous. It's a pity, you say. It's unfortunate, outrageous, heartbreaking. You make these declarations, which are partly true but mostly false, and life goes on.

But what also happens is that the images enter an aesthetic realm, detached from the human pain from which they emerged. It is too easy to forget Rosa Ramírez standing in her home, mourning as any of us would, and it is too easy to remember the striking photo of her dead son and granddaughter. The publication of such images is often followed by speculation about which among them is likely to win prizes. The photographer of the spectacularly terrible image is immediately congratulated by his or her peers, for some glory is surely on its way: a Pulitzer Prize perhaps, or a World Press Photo award. And this slope slips down to that everlouder demographic that exults in making America great again, among whom the brutal images do more direct work. The images show foreigners getting what they deserve; far from being an indictment, they portray a natural order. "Reality is don't be illegal," as one commenter on the *Times* site put it. Another wrote, "The bad judgment of the father in attempting to swim a river with a toddler on his back is his responsibility."

The weak and the disesteemed should suffer, and indeed they suffer. They should die, and indeed they die. The world is what it is. Not only is it easy to bear other people's misfortune, but their very suffering confirms that they are undeserving of mercy.

• • •

Photographs of extreme suffering will continue to be published; few publications will pass up the opportunity to feature a memorable image. If the past is any guide, they will be published in a way that does not particularly challenge those who wield the power of life and death over others. The *New York Times*, for instance, describing its decision to publish Le Duc's photograph, said it was careful not to make a "political statement" or convey "a position on the issue of immigration." This carefulness, in the face of horrific policy, already takes a position.

Nor is it likely that the asymmetry between those whose pain is turned into news and those who "consume" the news can be corrected. There are powerful, almost incontrovertible, codes of decorum maintained by and for people who are thought of as White, or who have been invited to participate in Whiteness. The racial disparity in published photographs of traumatized bodies is by now a recurring, and almost tedious, question. Media organizations have standard (and often grouchy) ripostes to the question each time it arises, usually involving an appeal to newsworthiness. And yet, newsworthiness rarely brings destroyed White bodies to the front page of the newspaper.

The questions we need to ask now are more urgent and more discomfiting. What sort of person needs to see such photographs in order to know what they should already know? Who are we if we need to look at ever more brutal images in order to feel something? What will be brutal enough?

These photographs, finally, are mirrors, not windows. We look into them, and what they reflect back to us is something monstrous and hard to reconcile with our notion of ourselves. We look, and look, and then—sated with looking, secure in our reactions, perennially missing the point—we put them away.

Shadow Cabinet:
On Kerry James Marshall

1

After Kerry James Marshall's *Portrait of the Artist as a Shadow of His Former Self* (1980), the shadow henceforth is no longer only an extension of the self, or a riff on it, or a mere variation on it. It is the self, and the self is the shadow.

Shadow and substance have played around each other for a long time. Since before Shakespeare wrote, "What is your substance, whereof are you made, / That millions of strange shadows on you tend?"

In Marshall's work, substance and shadow merge, as in a total eclipse, transfiguring the perceptual landscape.

2

Kora, a young woman in the Peloponnesian city-state of Sicyon, had a lover who was departing. To preserve his memory, she drew a careful and sinuous line around his shadow. (The account, taken to be the originary myth of portraiture, is recounted in book 35 of Pliny the Elder's *Naturalis historia*.) Kora's father, Butades, filled the outline of the shadow with clay and fired it alongside his pots.

A means of remembering what would otherwise have been forgotten. A shadow made permanent.

3

Have you ever heard anything so absurd? Africa, sun-stunned and light-inundated Africa, described as the "Dark Continent"? Something more than metaphor must be at play here. It must be some other darkness being displaced or reassigned.

The term "Dark Continent" became popular as part of the colonial enterprise in the nineteenth century, submerging and effacing thousands of years of interaction between Europe and Africa. This was the kind of distance colonialists needed. Something was being pretended at, a familiarity posing as lack of familiarity, some darkness that was a symbolic representation not of those so-named but of those who did the naming.

4

Marshall is looking for nothing. No. He is looking for what's not there. No, not quite. He is looking for what is there but not seen. Well, almost, try again. He is looking for what is there but not seen *by them*. That's it.

Marshall wants to, he says, "address absence with a capital A." Address, absence, a, A—that's how to begin an alphabet, an anecdote, an account.

5

A silhouette is a traced, mechanically drawn, or free-drawn shadow filled in with black. It might be an artistic shadow materially made of black, as in a cutout. This by-now ordinary word has a surprising origin: Étienne de Silhouette, a short-term finance minister to Louis XV in 1757, is its eponym. Silhouette was infamously stringent and cheap, and anything that was thought of as insubstantial or miserly was thus denoted as *à la Silhouette*.

Auguste Edouart, who settled in London in 1814, was a leading portraitist in black-paper profiles. He called himself "the black shade man." Skiagram, shadowgraph, shade, were some of the terms for his art, until Edouart helped popularize the now favored term: *silhouette*.

6

The popularity of photography after Louis Daguerre's announcement in 1839 inaugurated a loss of interest in silhouettes. But the public imagination was nevertheless haunted by the idea of fixing shadows, making them permanent. With the rise in popularity of *cartes de visite*, certain daguerreotypists urged their prospective clients to "secure the shadow 'ere the substance fade."

What they were calling for was not mere portraiture but, specifically, portraiture of the beloved recently dead. Life, on its way to forgetting, was detained one final time in postmortem portraits.

7

It got dark. "I am invisible, understand," the unnamed narrator says in *Invisible Man*, "simply because people refuse to see me." When he arrives at Liberty Paints, he's set to work mixing a shade of white called Optic White. Optic White is created by mixing the white foundation with ten drops of a particular black chemical. Thus mixed, Optic White comes out dazzlingly white: "If It's Optic White, It's the Right White." Dazzling white. The black is in there, though. *Address absence with a capital A.*

8

With what measure of innocence can a Black American encounter and absorb any display of prices or pricing? What shadow falls perpetually on sales, on selling, on those whose history is in part having been sold as goods are sold? The thought cannot be constantly overt—no one could live that way—but surely it irradiates any encounter with price, with pricing. Slavery was a profit-and-loss activity in living color.

In criminology and sociology, the amount of undiscovered or unreported crime is called the "dark figure."

9

"Yea, though I walk through the valley of the shadow of death, I will fear no evil." The psalmist speaks not of the valley of death but, in a surprising extension, of the valley of the *shadow* of death. Some Christian interpretation, such as that by Clement of Rome in 96 CE, has it as a prophecy of the journey of Christ through the valley of death. The phrase "shadow of death" recurs in the Hebrew Bible. In addition to Psalm 23, it is also found in Job 3:5, Isaiah 9:2, and elsewhere in the Psalms.

One rabbinic midrash reads "the valley of the shadow of death" as purgatory, a temporary state of torment that God will eventually alleviate. Another midrash, from the early medieval Midrash Tehillim, locates it in an actual space, the desert of Ziph, where David is fleeing his enemies Saul, Doeg, and Ahithophel.

But when the speaker implores God, in Psalm 17:8, "Keep me as the apple of the eye, hide me under the shadow of thy wings," the positive sense of the shadow emerges. The shadow then becomes a cooling place, a protection and bulwark, not a threat to be overmastered but a refuge in which to be enclosed.

10

In the shadow of a cave on the limestone plateau of the Ardèche River, by the light of flares and torches, responding with intuition and skill to the swells and dips of a rock face, human beings painted.

The images must have danced in the inconstant light of the torches: lions, bears, rhinoceroses, the animals of the real and dream worlds. These creatures, many of which are now extinct, were likely depicted for shamanistic purposes. Nearer the entrance of the cave, the painting was done with red ocher. Deeper inside, the preferred color was black, a black pigment from charcoal, soot, carbon black, the residue of fire. These early painters would return, bearing their torches, and the animals they had rendered in black would shimmer back to life again. Permanent shadows, thirty thousand years old, and from there grew and spread the complicated cultural possibility of black, simultaneously sacred, reviled, and beloved.

11

When I was a boy on the Dark Continent, everyone at my school, with the exception of one or two Indian kids, with the exception of the very rare White foreign student, was Black. This was in Lagos, and there was nothing dark about the continent.

We made fun of each others' appearances as children everywhere tend to do. We finely determined where on the light to dark spectrum each of us stood. Not that we cared either way who was light or who was dark. Thousands of miles from European or New World racism, we were interested in making fun of difference only for the sake of making fun. The lighter-skinned boys we called "yellow" or *oyinbo* (White person). Middle tones were not really named, since what is considered the standard needs no mockery.

The darker boys had a variety of names: "blackie" or *dudu* (Yoruba for "Black"). A good friend of mine, a dark-skinned boy, was "Big Stout." His sister, by the logic of the schoolyard, was "Small Stout." Big Stout was well loved and was also called, from time to time, "Shadow." As per: black shade man.

12

The chromatic value of a color is its relative lightness or darkness. This statement, which may be read in the obvious sociological ways, is also a statement of technical fact in painterly practice. The chromatic value of a color is distinct from its saturation or temperature.

Ivory black is black with a brown tint, a carbon black pigment; it was traditionally made of ivory but is now usually made from animal bones. Mars black has a denser tint and a neutral temperature. Lamp black is a bluish black.

"Black art," Faith Ringgold has said, "must use its own color black to create its own light, since that color is the most immediate black truth."

13

God made night and day, organized the distribution of shadow. The earth's shadow where it is not reached by the sun, the moon's shadow to determine what kind of night a night is. "The night has a love for throwing its shadows around a man / a bridge, a horse, the gun, a grave," wrote Charles Olson.

"Half our days we pass in the shadow of the earth," wrote Thomas Browne.

All continents are dark continents, half the time. But the darkness is not empty.

14

In 1815, Charles Catton the Younger, a landscape painter, was living and working on a Hudson River farm. Catton was displeased that his enslaved man Robert was visiting a young woman, also enslaved, on a neighboring farm. With his son's help, Catton beat Robert severely, almost to death.

Robert had been visiting Isabella (known as Bell). After the near-homicide by the Cattons, Robert and Bell were not allowed to see each other ever again. Robert died a few years later, and Bell remained haunted by the injustice all her life.

Some works by Catton are held at the Metropolitan Museum of Art and the Rijksmuseum.

Bell escaped from slavery in 1826. In 1843, she gave herself her own true name: Sojourner Truth.

15

Every painter is in the history of painting. What makes a given painter interesting, one of the things that gives a painter a chance to be interesting, is his or her sense of where he or she sits in the lineage of those who have painted. The painters too indebted to their forebears place themselves too early in the timeline, and their work has all the weakness of a nostalgic position. Those at the opposite extreme, whose work speaks only to the future, can only be judged by the future (and the future will find most of them wanting).

I am drawn to painters who are in a proper present tense, painters who have a well-calibrated relationship with what painting has been, who manifest what painting is and allow for what painting could come to be. Such artists are convincingly contemporary, their practices and gestures confirming their inheritance of the lineage. As custodians of the history of painting, they know their place in it. They are twice timely: just in time, and right on time.

16

In Kurosawa's *Kagemusha* (1980), the shogun dies and his advisors decide to keep the death secret. The shogun is replaced in ceremonial settings by a body double, a so-called shadow warrior. Gradually, something no less poignant for being predictable begins to happen: the shadow warrior begins to feel in himself the power and bodily authority of the real shogun. The shadow begins to act like the real body, to the astonishment and dismay of the courtiers. The shadow, one might say, eclipses the substance.

17

In Addis Ababa, I see Julie Mehretu's *Conjured Parts (Tongues)* (2016), a painting made with a host of black marks. The painting pulses with murmurs and possibilities. I am back in the Chauvet cave in 30,000 BCE; I am inside an Amharic manuscript; I am in a basement club festooned with graffiti; I am inside a forest at night during a rainstorm, a Twombly in negative, written and overwritten, a murky palimpsest. I am speaking in tongues.

Speaking of tongues: in Sri Lanka, eating the tongue of the thalagoya, a monitor lizard, as Michael Ondaatje writes in *Running in the Family*, is believed to give one the gift of eloquence.

18

The word "underpainting" brings technique to mind. The underpainting is one of the means by which a painter conveys his or her *disegno* onto the surface of the painting. It establishes the structures, contrasts, and tonal values that the overpainting will later accentuate.

The query "What is underpainting?" associatively suggests another, quite different query: "What is *under* painting?"

Or: "What is under the history of painting?"

19

Rembrandt's 1632 painting *Jean Pellicorne with His Son Caspar* is at the Wallace Collection in London. In the dual portrait, the father wears all black, save for his white lace neck ruff and sleeves, and the son, about four years old, wears brown. The painting is in the detailed and somewhat glassy style of Rembrandt's paintings from the early 1630s, after he moved to Amsterdam from Leiden, the period when he fully came into his own as a master painter and garnered excited patronage.

In the painting, Jean Pellicorne, a rich merchant, receives a bag of money from his infant son; the painting symbolizes filial duty. It demonstrates the hope that someday Caspar will be wealthy, too, and will provide for the family. The lesson is underscored by the image faintly visible in the background, the biblical story of the young Samuel being dedicated to the Lord.

Caspar Pellicorne did indeed become very wealthy, in part by trafficking enslaved people. In 1677, for instance, he signed, along with others, a contract to supply eighteen hundred enslaved people to the Spanish West Indies.

20

When a doctor places an X-ray on the screen, we hold our breath. Something significant is about to be shown. The flicking of the X-ray onto the screen is a calling to attention. Our untrained eyes cannot interpret this cluster of shadow, but to the doctor's eye, the shadows are legible. Some of them could be malign or, if there be mercy, all of them could be "unremarkable."

David Hammons's *Injustice Case* (1970), a body print in gri-
saille, presents like an X-ray. This dark figure, remarkable, framed
by the American flag, sees through what is not seen *by them*.

21

Kerry James Marshall's *Untitled (Underpainting)* (2018) is a color-
istic field of blacks and browns (plate 4). It depicts Black people
in the space of a museum gallery. The gallery is seen from two
perspectives.

Painting is essentially flat on the surface, even allowing for im-
pasto. It works two-dimensionally and either actively courts illusion or actively subverts it. *Untitled (Underpainting)* does both,
placing itself in dialogue with paintings about looking by Veláz-
quez (a master of black), Vermeer, Courbet, Manet (another
master of black), and with previous work by Marshall himself.

But *Untitled (Underpainting)* does more. It addresses a different kind of illusion: what is under painting, the black that has
been there all along, but not seen *by them*.

22

In 1875, Eadweard Muybridge boarded a steamship and headed
to Panama. He had just been acquitted of shooting dead Major
Harry Larkyns, his wife's lover. (The killing was ruled a justifiable
homicide.) During this exile, he also went to Costa Rica, Honduras, El Salvador, Guatemala, and Mexico. His famous studies
of animal locomotion still lay in the future.

The glass-plate photographic emulsions used by nineteenth-
century photographers were hypersensitive to blue light. This
meant that skies were often washed out, white, in the print. Photographers frequently combined two or more exposures in the
making of a final print — one for the landscape, and another, with

a shorter exposure time, for the sky—to allow for detail in both sections. Muybridge was a virtuoso of this technique, and often placed an unrelated sky above a landscape. His pictures thus ended up being fictions that exist on paper, with only a faint relationship to the real world.

Cloud studies especially preoccupied him during his Central American sojourn. How could the fugitive detail and subtlety of these white clouds be properly registered? Again and again, Muybridge went at the problem, creating an album of shaded whites.

23

In the West Indies—as V. S. Naipaul notes in *The Middle Passage* (1962)—the gradations of skin color were stringently and absurdly ordered: "white, fusty, musty, dusty, tea, coffee, cocoa, light black, black, dark black."

24

A black soft-sided quadrilateral with a bluish tint advancing, or receding, in a field of black with a purple or neutral tint: in his late paintings, Rothko attempted to evoke and even assert the sublime. Black became for him what white was for Muybridge in his cloud-chasing days: a full spectrum of tonal possibility. His intimation was that there was a lot to see inside black, though most of what he saw was the valley of the shadow of death. Rothko inhabited the sorrowful wing of black's possibility. The pictures were not generative, or consoling, or joyful.

25

A talk given by Toni Morrison in 1975 draws my attention to the dispassionate language and affect of certain historical documents. This affect is palpable particularly in those documents that concern themselves with profit. She cites *The Historical Statistics of the United States from Colonial Times to 1957*. In section Z, which addresses "Colonial and Pre-Federal Statistics," some of the itemized sections are as follows:

— Coal exported from James River ports in Virginia, by destination, 1758–1765
— Pig iron exported to England, by colony, 1723–1776
— Bar iron imported from England, by American Colonies, 1710–1750
— Value of furs exported to England, by British Continental Colonies, 1700–1775
— Indigo and silk exported from South Carolina and Georgia, 1747–1788
— Value of commodity exports and imports, earnings and value of slaves imported into British North American Colonies, 1768–1772
— Rice exported from Charleston, S.C., by destination, 1717–1766
— Pitch, tar, and turpentine exported from Charleston, S.C., 1725–1774

Coal. Pig iron. Bar iron. Furs. Indigo and silk. Slaves. Rice. Pitch, tar, and turpentine.

I'm haunted by the word "profit." I am lost when I contemplate "value." Their meanings slip from my grip.

The "dark figure."

26

Man in a Window (1978) by Roy DeCarava is dense with black information. The man in the photograph is black, the curtains around the window are black, the room in which he sits is black, the light that emanates from the scene is black. One might be inclined to read them as different shades of gray, but this image, like so many by DeCarava, is multivocally black. Out of those black tones, the form rises to the surface in relation, consolation, and recognition.

There's both magic and lineage in this window. Beyte Saar's *Black Girl's Window* (1969) echoes to one side of it. Kerry James Marshall's untitled 2018 painting (a Black girl seen through a black-framed window) echoes to the other. Timeliness is being in time and on time. Work conversant with the history of art, and in conversation with it, is timely.

27

From 1864 onward, Sojourner Truth owned the copyright of her *cartes de visite*, on which she printed the legend: "I Sell the Shadow, to Support the Substance."

These images were used to raise funds for antislavery causes. Truth sold the Shadow (the photograph of herself) to support the Substance (her own substantial body, and the substantive cause of abolition). Contrast the commercial daguerreotypists' "Secure the shadow 'ere the substance fade" with Truth's "I Sell the Shadow, to Support the Substance": it is the difference between working around death and working for life.

I *sell*. The one who was sold (sold at an auction when she was nine years old for one hundred dollars, along with a flock of sheep) now has the agency to sell. *I* sell. But where the body was sold, it is now the image, the idea, that is sold, to support the body. This is an ethic that connects vision with liberty.

28

"Blackness is non-negotiable in those pictures," Marshall says.
Black with yellow ocher. Black with raw umber. Black with a
certain blue. Black with another kind of blue. Carbon black, from
soot. Mars black, from iron oxide. Ivory black, from burned white
bone. Black, black, black, black, black, black, black. Seven different kinds, an infinity.

Nighted Color:
On Lorna Simpson

Blues, dark teal, deep purple, black. A fully clothed woman sleeps in bed, her arms in the uncalculated attitude of the unconscious. Another woman stands on a ledge, on the verge of endangering her own life or of saving it. Then the same figures, fragmented and rearranged, their colors flowing into one another, repeat across the five sections of a nearly twenty-one-foot span, intensifying the sensation of physical precarity and dream logic. *Montage*, Lorna Simpson's work of photography, screen print, and painting, was one of the featured pictures in her 2018 London gallery show, *Unanswerable*. It's an apt title. Simpson's work, which often suspends meaning even while seeming to promise resolution, has long had something productively elusive about it.

Her first notable successes were photographs paired with texts. The photos were black and white, simple, and direct, usually of a single female figure, often seen from the back. The texts, far from resolving the image, were suggestive and inconclusive. In *Waterbearer* (1986), a woman in a plain white shift dress pours water from two vessels, a plastic jug in one hand, a metal ewer in the other. She's turned away from us. The text below the photograph, rendered in all caps, reads, "SHE SAW HIM DISAPPEAR BY THE RIVER, THEY ASKED HER TO TELL WHAT HAPPENED, ONLY TO DISCOUNT HER MEMORY." What has happened here? Who is "she" and who "him" and who "they"? It is as though we've been thrust into a detective story containing only the faintest trace of the original incident. All that remains is a parable of a woman who is not believed. *Waterbearer*, in its radical simplicity, crosses a distance of more than three decades to comment on current affairs.

Like *Waterbearer*, many other works of Simpson's from that period—including *Twenty Questions (A Sampler)* (1986), *Five Day Forecast* (1988), and *7 Mouths* (1993)—are both figurative and fragmentary. Evenly lit, crisply photographed, they look like pictures from an illustrated medical dictionary, indexical images of heads, torsos, and mouths that are detached from context. Even in a work like *Figure* (1991), the figure in question—sheathed in a black dress and set in the black infinity of no particular place— feels like a fragment, as though she had been extracted from a group photo or a furnished room. The texts accompanying her, eight engraved plastic plaques, read like excerpts from a language primer: "figured the worst," "he was disfigured," "figured there would be no reaction," and so on. Here, not only has the story been winnowed down; it is in fact completely gone. There's no story. We are left with only the tensions of concrete poetry.

Sometime in the mid-1990s, Simpson began to detect clichéd responses to her work. At the same time, her own thinking was evolving. What does an image of a Black woman mean? A commentary on race? An assertion about gender? Simpson branched out from figure-based images and began to experiment more with varied subject matter—landscapes, inanimate objects like wigs—

and also with unusual quasi-sculptural material like felt and standing screens. A series of monumental photographic polyptychs, several of them landscapes, collectively titled *Public Sex* (1995–1998) and featuring no figures at all, addressed the provocative title only obliquely. These pictures, made over many years, contain what Okwui Enwezor called "the rumor of the body." Mysteries of a jagged and deadpan sort, they would go on to influence the noirish tone of Simpson's later film work.

Simpson began to set ever more intricate conceptual layers between her initial inspiration for a work and the finished product. The idea for *9 Props* (1995) began during a residency at the Pilchuck Glass School in Washington where, with the aid of artisans at the school, she fabricated a series of dark vessels modeled on vases and other objects used in the portrait work of the pioneering Harlem photographer James Van Der Zee. But these vessels were not themselves the final work. She shipped them back to New York and then photographed them against a plain background. And that still was not the work. Further intervention followed: she turned those photographic images into nine lithographs, which she printed on felt. Finally, she wrote captions below each lithographed vessel, describing the context in which it originally appeared. One of them, for instance, reads:

Dinner Party with boxer Harry Wills,

1926

James VanDerZee

Harry Wills a k a "The Black Panther," boxer, businessman- sits with seven other men and women, mostly women with champagne glasses raised as a woman on his left makes a toast in his honor. There are three bottles of champagne, a crystal decanter, a bottle of port, an arrangement of flowers and fruit, and before each guest an untouched china place setting.

From multiple directions, the work gestures at what cannot be seen: the original placement of the vessels that inspired Simpson's own, the people in the photographs by James Van Der Zee, the social life of Harlem evoked by his photographs and the complexity of manners and class implied by them. All that vanished world of culture and experience is reduced to an elegant grid, as simple as an antiquarian's catalog, a thought picture that demands calm engagement and imaginative intervention on the viewer's part. Without being representational, it is about race, but not "race" off in some category by itself, hemmed in only by questions of skin color, separate from life.

■ ■ ■

"Represent!" in the Black American sense means standing up for your people, expressing solidarity, and letting a shared ethos underwrite your presence and work. It is an exhortation, a greeting, and a farewell. The word also has more conventional associations in the visual arts: as mimesis, in contrast with the abstract or the symbolic. To represent, in this more common sense, is to make work that visually corresponds to realities out there in the world, to illustrate uncomplicatedly. This second sense of "represent" is enjoying a vogue in the art world. Realism is back. This is mostly welcome: after so long an absence of Black figures and Black faces in art museums, they are now being seen more frequently. Many artists, Black and otherwise, are depicting the Black body. It is necessary and, often enough, artistically successful. Yet just as often, maybe more often, it fails. The galleries are full of unobjectionable, unmemorable representations, work that offers little more than a clumsy shorthand for social concern.

A strong appeal of Simpson's work is that she has always embraced the inherent complexity of Blackness, her own Blackness as well as the Blackness that runs ineluctably through American history. She does not reject representational depictions, but neither does she feel the need to confine herself only to "race" work. When an artist uses a Black model, she is presenting a human question by foregrounding a human presence. Is a White man a person while a Black woman is and can only be a gendered and racialized subject? As Kellie Jones has pointed out, nonwhite bodies are often thought of as "not neutral enough for the dispassionate formulas thought to constitute conceptual practice." If a Black woman's race and gender are the only things apparent to a certain viewer, Simpson seems to say, the ethical responsibility to escape those shackles is the viewer's.

Freedom is Lorna Simpson's starting point and her permanent theme. A humane current animates all of her work, which is simultaneously about the "neutral" space of ideas and the particularized experience of the body. This recent work, *Montage*, is photographic and painterly, a riff on a pair of found photographs, sequenced to look like a giant strip of film (plate 5). It deals with dreams and nightmares, ambiguities and vulnerabilities, at the heart of which is what Simpson calls "the push and pull of photography": the stuttering potential inherent in mechanical reproduction and the imperfect registrations that mirror subconscious life. It is a rapid response to the current political climate, situating a crucial part of it in the most intimate space of all, where the hectoring "they" is temporarily held at bay in favor of the puzzled "I."

In your own sleeping bed, images persist and words are hard to come by. You are immersed in dream hues and nighted color. This is the art we need now: rich, allusive, tongue-tied, and unanswerable.

The Blackness
of the Panther

I began to become African almost thirty years ago. That was when
I left Nigeria and moved to the United States. I had been born in
the US in the summer of 1975 and taken to Nigeria in the fall of
the same year. For the next seventeen years, Nigeria was home.
But I also knew I was American, that the US was a kind of home
too, because I had been born there. But was I African? I didn't feel
it. What I felt was that I was a Lagos boy, a speaker of Yoruba, a
citizen of Nigeria. The Africans were those other people, some of
whom I read about in books, or had seen wearing tribal costumes
in magazines, or encountered in weird fictional form in movies.

In the summer of 1992, that began to change. The US provided
a contrast to my latent Africanness. "What are you?" "I'm Nigerian." "Where are you from, man?" "Lagos." "Leggo my Eggo?"
No one had heard of Lagos. I was African; that was the kind of
"other" I was. It was news to me, but I didn't fight back for long. I
fell in with others who were in a similar predicament, and began
to learn African.

. . .

I sometimes feel in my body a paradoxical loss: the loss of forgetting. I find myself longing for an earlier time when what I knew was contingent and always sheltered by what I didn't know. Knowledge, in the days before instantaneous electronic recall, was full of potential energy. It was attended by a guesswork that fostered a different way of knowing, one that allowed for ranges rather than insisting on points.

Here is an attempt to struggle to remember: I know, or knew, a few things about the big cats. Lions are found on the Serengeti, tigers in South Asia. Both are enormous. Cheetahs are the fastest, obviously; leopards, good climbers, dragging their prey up a tree. Both are African (animals can be African, but only people can be *Africans*). I think the scientific names of the big cats contain "Panthera," though I can't be sure. I refuse, for the sake of this exercise, to check. *Panthera leo.* That's lions, I think. Jaguars look like leopards but are of stockier and more compact build. They're South American. This is where it gets cloudier. Are panthers jaguars? Or are they their own thing? If panthers are monochrome jaguars, then they can't be African, because jaguars are South American. Is a black panther the same thing as a black leopard? And what the fuck is a puma? What are mountain lions? I think they're the same as pumas: aren't they the North American ones? Wait, what about cougars?

I was into the big cats as a kid. Knew my cats back then, and freelanced in birds of prey (eagles, hawks, falcons, ospreys), which had a similarly complex family structure. Dabbled in dinosaurs too, but not seriously. I don't mind that I have now lost much of my taxonomic memory of these peak predators. What's sad is that, in the blink of an eye, I can look it all up.

. . .

On the morning of October 11, 1933, six years before the beginning of the European war in which Switzerland was to play a tangential but troubling role, the cage of the black panther at the Zürich Zoologischer Garten was found empty. The animal, a recent arrival from Sumatra, had escaped in the night. In the weeks that followed, numerous sightings were reported. The normally unflappable citizens of Zürich were caught up in hysteria. There were hundreds of articles in the Swiss press. Traps were set, and a few half-wild dogs were caught. Tracks thought to be those of the panther also turned out to belong to dogs. It was suggested by some that an exorcism be performed by the members of a religious cult. Someone else wrote to say that what was needed was a clairvoyant.

It wasn't until the middle of December, ten weeks after her escape, that the panther was found hiding under a barn in the boundary between the Zürich Oberland and the Canton of St. Gallen. The remains of roe deer found nearby were a clue as to how she had survived a Swiss winter. The black panther was discovered by a casual laborer, who immediately shot and killed her for food.

· · ·

Many movies made by Hollywood have engaged in thought experiments about Africa. Some, made for American Whites, resurrect colonial fantasy ("I had a farm in Africa"), with the African roles either brutish or naive. Others, made for American Blacks, have a goal of uplift, cloaking the African experience with a fictional grandeur. These fantasies, of either kind, are inevitably simplifications. There are fifty-four African countries. What would it mean to dream with these countries? What would it mean to dream with Mozambique, Sudan, Togo, or Libya, to think about their politics in all their hectic complexities? What would it look like to use what already exists as a narrative frame, even for works of fiction? Wakanda is a monarchy, and so is Zamunda. Why are monarchies the narrative default? Can we dream beyond royalty?

· · ·

Only once have I ever owned a pet: a cat, more than a decade ago. Her name was Mirabai, also known as Midnight. She'd leap up to meet me, this beautiful panther in miniature. Or she would go deep into prayer, as cats do, or knead some patch of sun on the wooden floor. But I could not train this sweet, playful, all-black kitten not to bite. I soon tired of having to take a course of anti-biotics each time she bit me. Three times she bit me, and twice visitors. There was no hostility there, she simply didn't know how to modulate, and often drew blood. More seriously, I discovered that I have a severe allergy to cat hair. Not all cats, but most. I hadn't known. Poor Mirabai. I had to return her to the shelter. But in my heart of hearts, I'm a cat person. I can stand dogs, but I more naturally like what cats do and how cats be.

· · ·

On my way to becoming African, I also began to become Black, which proved a more complex journey. "African" had been about mutual spaces with Africans: friends from across the continent, or people with whom I'd been placed in the same category. It had something to do with finding ourselves strangers in the strange American land, but also with our shared experience of the background radiation of colonialism. The formalized White supremacy of colonial rule ended in Nigeria only fifteen years be-fore I was born. It was still fresh. "African," whatever else it was, was about collectively undoing this assault.

"Black" was something else. It was, in a sense, more inclusive. In the inclusive sense, it took in all that colonial hangover and added to it the American experiences of slavery, slave rebellion, Jim Crow, and contemporary racism, as well as the connective tissue that bound the Black Atlantic into a single pulsing bruise—which brought all of the Caribbean into its orbit—as well as European, Latin American, and global diasporic Blackness.

But "Black" was also more restrictive because, in everyday language, "Black" (or "black") was American Black, and "American Black" meant American Black descended from enslaved people. It wasn't about every Black person in the world; it was localized to the American situation. To be Black in America, that localized tenor of "Black" had to be learned; it had to be learned and loved. Black skin (sometimes just a shade or two off-white) was the admission to the classroom, but Black American cultural codes were the lesson. So, I learned Black, like Obama learned Black, like Black British living in LA learn Black, like Jamaicans in Brooklyn, Haitians in Miami, Eritreans in DC, and Gambians in the Bronx learn Black. We learned Black and loved Black—knowing all the while, though, that it wasn't the only Black.

. . .

A landlocked nation, small and peaceful. The inhabitants are thought to be a simple, unostentatious people. But this is one of the richest nations on earth, and one of the most technologically advanced. The country is set at a great height, ringed by mountains. Its political system is stable. There have been no internal wars for centuries. Fearful of the mayhem convulsing the world, its citizens stay out of international disputes and do not open their borders to migrants. But behind the quiet-looking walls is a remarkable industriousness in the fields of scientific research, weapons development, and pharmaceutical innovation. The country has solved the mystery of transportation: traffic congestion is unknown there, and high-speed trains silently crisscross the territory. Now, in a rapidly changing world, the inhabitants of this country must decide if they want to continue hiding themselves from the world, or if they wish finally to take more responsibility and use their wealth and technology to improve the lot of others.

I'm talking about Switzerland, obviously. But Switzerland is a democracy. Wakanda, not so much. My antipathy to monarchies is intense, inflexible, and probably irrational. The hereditary right to rule offends me almost personally, whether I encounter it in fiction or in reality. I rate it, as ideas go, somewhere between eugenics and phrenology. Human history is full of monarchs. Let's leave them where most of them are, in the past. The societies I dream organize themselves around well-informed democratic choice. The dream extends past even the nation-state. No kings, no queens, no royal presidents, no dynasties. Temperamentally, I'm a regicide.

The nations and cities of Africa, as they are now, are each so consumed with the complexity of being their distinct selves from day to day that they cannot take on the thankless task of also being Hollywood's "Africa." African countries have always been in conversation with the world: an isolationist Blackness is incoherent and impossible: we already *been* cosmopolitan. In the modern world, Black is as unimaginable without White as White is unimaginable without Black. What we are is shaped by the other, for better or worse (for us, mostly worse), but the interaction is real. The way out is through. We can't wish that away, not even as a storytelling fantasy.

As for African kings, they exist even now, but they mostly

occupy modest roles, at the level of the ethnic group or clan rather than as potentates over nation-states. These lesser kings have ceremonial roles within larger political organizations. They know their place, answering to state governors or local government chairpersons. Meanwhile, the few real national monarchies that remain are nothing to be envied. They're absurd throwbacks, no kind of future.

Truth is not stranger than fiction, but it is more specific, more contradictory, more hectic. "Africa"—vague or composite— cannot hope to match the complexity or interest of any actual place in Africa.

. . .

In the winter of 1902, Rainer Maria Rilke visited the zoo at the Jardins des plantes in Paris, and there he saw a black panther. The poem he wrote in response, the earliest of his *Neue Gedichte*, is one of his most famous:

Sein Blick ist vom Vorübergehn der Stäbe
so müd geworden, daß er nichts mehr hält.
Ihm ist, als ob es tausend Stäbe gäbe
und hinter tausend Stäben keine Welt.

Der weiche Gang geschmeidig starker Schritte,
der sich im allerkleinsten Kreise dreht,
ist wie ein Tanz von Kraft um eine Mitte,
in der betäubt ein großer Wille steht.

Nur manchmal schiebt der Vorhang der Pupille
sich lautlos auf—Dann geht ein Bild hinein,

geht durch der Glieder angespannte Stille —
und hört im Herzen auf zu sein.

In my rapid translation:

His gaze, from the constant passing of the bars,
becomes so tired that it can no longer hold anything.
He feels as though there are a thousand bars
and behind the thousand bars, no world.

The soft strong supple steps
that turn in the smallest circle
are like a ritual dance in the middle of which
stands a great stunned will.

Only sometimes does the curtain of the pupil
soundlessly lift. Then a picture enters,
goes through the tensed silence of the limbs,
and, entering the heart, ceases to be.

Rilke's poetry, at its best, is a marvel of sympathy. He can ghost himself into the lives of things, adopt the view from their perspective. The panther in his poem is black because of the color of its coat. But it is also a racialized subject.

All black panthers are black in color, and none can now evade cultural meaning: the caged cat, the escaped cat, the never-captured cat, the Black people who are seen as animals, the '60s comic-book hero, the radical political party, the twenty-first-century film stars. All black panthers and Black Panthers are black, black like night and also Black like me.

No translation of Rilke's "Der Panther" is entirely satisfying, so dependent is the poem on the propulsive rhythms of the German original. Only a version will do, one full of forgettings, misreadings, a stealth leap into the poem, an ambush:

> A thousand bars flicker in front of nothing.
> A thousand bars — his exhausted eyes can't take it.
> Soft paws, supple tread. He circles, dazed.
> But sometimes! The eyes slide open, an image enters, goes
>   through the tense limbs, and, on reaching the heart, vanishes.

· · ·

In addition to big cats and soaring raptors, in childhood I was keen on Transformers, Voltron, Speed Racer, and a number of American superhero comic books. This was in Lagos in the 1980s. By the time I was in my midteens, I had lost interest in all that: sci fi, fantasy, video games, comics, cartoons. There are exceptions: I like *Solaris, 2001: A Space Odyssey, Children of Men, Minority Report*, but that's a fairly narrow selection of dystopian futurism. I love Sun Ra's *Space Is the Place*, but that's something else entirely.

But the recent leotard-and-cape blockbusters that dominate earnings in Hollywood bore me. It faintly feels like a terrible thing to admit (what kind of monster doesn't love superhero movies?), but the world is made of what we're into and what we're not into, and there's consolation in knowing what's yours. In certain genres I do not love, the louder genres especially, there's so much at stake that it can feel there's therefore nothing at stake. The fate of the planet, the destiny of the universe, and so on are always one clever decision or heroic battle away. The fight sequences stretch on, but the fights don't really feel like fights. Compare a battle in any recent big-budget superhero film to one in a Kurosawa samurai epic like *Ran*: the recent films are all CGI, while Kurosawa feels like steel and flesh and dust and actual battlefield clamor. In a typical superhero film, enemies are killed in great numbers, but death is curiously light, inconsequential, undeathly. (In *Black Panther*, what would the climactic civil war in Wakanda have felt like had there been a serious reckoning with its death toll? It would have made apparent the movie's discomfiting secret: that it has two lead villains and no hero.)

Maybe it's a tonal thing, or maybe it's economic censorship—inescapable in any film that costs more than $100 million to make, and even less forgiving than ideological censorship: that money must be recouped, and there must be profit. Or maybe it's that the films are made, as all films are, for those who love them, not for those who doubt them. I know I'm an outlier. The box office returns of the Marvel Cinematic Universe prove that heretical disrespecters of the superhero money-laundering operation are outnumbered. But even for us, there can be the fine surprise, for example, of a film that strains at those conventions, attempts to establish new mythologies, and in the process invites even nonpartisans to think with its world, reactionary as that world might be. Coogler did that.

. . .

On a rainy Tuesday afternoon in March 2015, I visited the Parque Zoológico de São Paulo. Zoos often echo early science and colonial practice. I like to visit the zoo in various places because a zoo can often feel like the opening chapter of a given country. It's as though the logic of a society's organization has been reduced to fundamentals in a zoo, a delimited setting where one finds the rulers and the ruled, types and typologies, symbols everywhere and meaning nowhere.

That day in São Paulo, I saw elephants, giraffes, a strange fox-like dog, chimpanzees, flamingos, a boa constrictor. There were few solitary adults around, but there were a couple of boisterous school groups. Perhaps this is one place where my tastes do reliably overlap with those of younger children. I go to zoos, and while I'm there, I'm thinking about what a zoo means—it is both defensible and indefensible—but I'm also absorbed by the gallimaufric variety and sheer strangeness of those other beings on the other side of the barrier. Their gazes, dulled by human encounter, can no longer admit us into their existential circle but, like tarnished mirrors, those gazes still glimmer from time to time with recognition.

I do not recall now why I paused by the black panther's cage that day. I began to record a brief video on my phone. Soft paws, supple tread. She (or he) moved swiftly, worriedly. It was an intent rather than distracted pacing. He (or she) was simultaneously gorgeous and frantic, loping, maddened, a grievously confined power.

· · ·

In 1902, some four years before he wrote "Der Panther," Rilke had written another poem, "Die Aschanti," about a group of West African men and women. They had been displayed in the zoolike setting of the Jardin d'acclimatation in Paris. The practice of exhibiting African people (as well as Samoans, Inuit, and Sami) in zoos, circuses, and world fairs, was especially rampant between the late nineteenth century and 1930. The history of this atrocity is deep, but a signal instance was the case of Saartjie Baartman, who was brought from South Africa to England in 1810 and put on display in London.

In the 1870s, in the name of ethnographic research, there were human zoos in Antwerp, Paris, Barcelona, Hamburg, London, Milan, and New York City. The Congolese Ota Benga was confined to the monkey house at the Bronx Zoo in 1906, and freed only on the protestations of African American activists. (He would kill himself a decade later, with a gunshot to the heart. To the heart!) And in 1930, three years before the black panther escaped from the Zürich Zoologischer Garten, a group of Senegalese people had been put on display there, in Zürich.

"Die Aschanti" is a poem of disappointment. Rilke finds that the Ashanti are not African enough for him, not savage enough. One verse goes:

Keine wilde fremde Melodie.
Keine Lieder, die vom Blute stammten,
und kein Blut, das aus den Tiefen schrie.

In Edward Snow's translation:

No wild unheard-of melodies.
No songs which issued from the blood,
and no blood which screamed out from the depths.

It goes on. There are "no brown girls who stretched out / velvety in tropical exhaustion," "no eyes which blaze like weapons," no mouths "broad with laughter." The Ashanti are just there, self-possessed, with a "bizarre" vanity, acting almost as though they were equal to Europeans. "And it made me shudder seeing that," Rilke writes. He can only conclude the poem by declaring, "O how much truer are the animals / that pace up and down in steel grids."

That's racist.

. . .

Eusébio da Silva Ferreira, born in Maputo to a poor family during Portuguese colonial rule, moved to Portugal and became the
greatest of Benfica's players, and perhaps the greatest ever to
have worn Portugal's shirt, for greatness is more than a matter of
trophies and goal tallies. Eusébio was black and beautiful on the
field, quick, quick, in that red shirt of his, blessed with a tremendous right-footed shot. He was the best player in the 1966 World
Cup. This man of feline reflexes was called the King, the Black
Pearl, and, above all, "la Pantera Negra," the Black Panther (as was
the boxer Harry Wills, more than half a century earlier). Perhaps
it is only too obvious that the first great football player from the
African continent would be compared to an animal, but it is also
true that neither the panther nor the player is diminished by the
comparison, which after all seeks to put into words a beauty that
the heart cannot contain.

. . .

Had to look it up. Forgetting is impossible. It turns out a black
panther is two different animals, and no animal at all. It is no animal at all in the sense that a panther is not a distinct scientific
species. It is two different animals because a jaguar with a black
coat is a black panther, and a leopard with a black coat is a black
panther. The blackness of the panther, in the case of the jaguar,
is due to a dominant gene for coat coloration. The blackness of
the panther, in the case of the leopard, is due to a recessive gene.
Both are melanistic variants and when deh mutated gene for the
bleck color is expressed, deh big cat receives the powa of deh
Bleck Pentha.

. . .

Listen to Toni Morrison a second:

> Saying something is pitch black is like saying something is green.
> What kind of green? Green like my bottles? Green like a grass-
> hopper? Green like a cucumber, lettuce, or green like the sky just
> before it breaks loose to storm? Well, night black is the same way.
> May as well be a rainbow.

I learned Black, and I learned diversity in Blackness. Turns out
Black is multifarious and generative. It is capacious and dissent-
ing. Those who have to learn Black also expand what Black can
be. My pain is Black pain, my joy is Black joy, my individuality is
Black. I arc blackly in the rainbow with all the rest of those pitch-
black cats. Next person comes along to learn Black will have to
learn me too.

. . .

At least once a day, I think: "another world is possible." There's
life yet in our dreams. The pan-African political project is still
alive. The memory of whatever was good in the Bandung Conference or the Organization of African Unity still makes the heart
race. Flashes of common cause among the Darker Nations can be
illuminating and sustaining. But "Africa" as trope and trap, backdrop and background, interests me ever less.

I am more fascinated by Nairobi than by Africa, just as I am
more intrigued by Milan than by Europe. The general is where
solidarity begins, but the specific is where our lives come into
proper view. I don't want to hear "Africa" unless it's a context in

which someone would also say "Asia" or "Europe." Ever notice how real Paris is? That's how real I need Lagos to be. Folks can talk about Paris all day without once generalizing about Europe. I want to talk about Lagos, not about Africa. I want to hear someone speaking Yoruba, Ewe, Tiv, or Lingala. "African" is not a language. I want to know if a plane is going to the Félix-Houphouët-Boigny International Airport or the O. R. Tambo International Airport. You can't go to "Africa," fam. Africa is almost twelve million square miles. I want to be particular about being particular about what we are talking about when we talk about Africa.

. . .

I grew up with Black presidents, Black generals, Black kings, Black heroes, both invented and real. Black thieves too, Black fools. It was Nigeria, biggest Black nation on earth. I shared a city with Fela Kuti for seventeen years. Everyone was Black! I've seen so many Black people my retina's black.

But, against the high-gloss white of anti-Black America, Blackness visible is a relief and a riot. That is something you learn when you learn Black. Marvel? Disney? Please. I won't belabor the obvious. But Black visibility, Black enthusiasm (in a time of death), Black spectatorship, and Black skepticism: where we meet is where we meet.

Going on twenty-nine years now. I learned African and am mostly over it. But what is that obdurate and versatile substance formed by tremendous pressure? What is "vibranium"? Too simple to think of it as a metal and tie it to a resource curse. Could it be something less palpable? Could it be a stand-in for Blackness itself, Blackness as an embodied riposte to anti-Blackness, a quintessence of mystery, resilience, self-containedness, and irreducibility?

Escape! I would rather be in the wild. I would rather be in a civilization of my own making, bizarre, contrary, as vain as that of the Whites, exterior to their logic. I'm always scoping the exits. "Drapetomania," they called it, in *Diseases and Peculiarities of the Negro Race* (1851), the irrepressible desire in certain enslaved people to run away.

. . .

Ten years pass and I still dream about that cat. The eyes slide open, an image enters. Where are you now, Mirabai? Euthanized years ago by the animal shelter? Or successfully adopted and now gracefully aging in some home in Brooklyn? With people, young or old, merciful and just? Dream cat, leaping up to meet me.

Restoring the Darkness

I first saw the photograph some years ago, online. Later, I tracked it down to its original source: *In Afric's Forest and Jungle; or, Six Years among the Yorubans*, a memoir published in 1899 by the Reverend R. H. Stone (figure 6). It shows a crowd in what is now Nigeria, but was then Yorubaland under British colonial influence. The caption below the photograph reads: "A king of Ejayboo. — Governor of Lagos on right. For years the rulers of this fierce tribe made the profession of Christianity a capital crime." This description is familiar in tone from the anthropological literature of the period, though the photograph is hard to date precisely. "Ejayboo" is what we would nowadays spell as "Ijebu," a subgroup of Yoruba. That catches my attention: I am Yoruba and also Ijebu, or at least from people who speak Ijebu. This picture is a time capsule from a world to which I am connected but had not seen before, a world by colonial encounter.

By the middle of the nineteenth century, through treaties and threats of force, the British had wrested control of Lagos, which is a coastal city, from its king. They then turned their efforts to improving access to the goods and services in the Yoruba hinter-

FIGURE 6. Anon., "A king of Ejayboo." From the Rev. R. H. Stone's memoir *In Afric's Forest and Jungle; or, Six Years among the Yorubans* (1899). Schomburg Center for Research in Black Culture. Photograph: New York Public Library, New York (https:// digitalcollections.nypl.org/items/510d47df-94d6-a3d9-e040-e00a18064a99).

land. The Yoruba were already by that time a populous and diverse ethnic group, full of rivalrous kingdoms large and small, some friendly to the British, others less so.

Stone, a Virginian sent by the Southern Baptist Convention, lived among them—lived among *us*—for two spells, in 1859–1863 and 1867–1869, which is to say, before, during, and after the American Civil War. He had this to say about Yoruba people: "They are reasonable, brave and patriotic, and are capable of a very high degree of intellectual culture." It is praise, but must be understood in the context of a statement he makes earlier in his book about living "among the barbarous people" of that part of the world. In any case, the Ijebu in the mid-nineteenth century were largely wealthy traders and farmers who did not want to give the British right of way to the interior of the country; only through diplomacy, subterfuge, and violence were they finally overcome.

The photograph in Stone's book was made in the aftermath. The White governor of Lagos—based on the plausible dates, it is probably John Hawley Glover—sits under an enormous umbrella. On one side of him is another high-ranking colonial officer. On the other side is the Ijebu king, or oba, probably the Awujale of the Ijebu kingdom, Oba Ademuyewo Fidipote. The oba wears a beaded crown, but the beads have been parted and his face is visible. This is unusual, for the oba is like a god and must be concealed when in public. The beads over his face, with their interplay of light and shadow, are meant to give him a divine aspect. Why is his face visible in this photograph? Some contravention of customary practice has taken place. The dozens of men seated on the ground in front of him are visibly alarmed. Many have turned their bodies away from the oba, and several are positioned toward the camera, not in order to look at the camera but in order to avoid looking at the exposed radiance of their king.

. . .

After the invention of the daguerreotype was announced in 1839, photography spread like wildfire. It became a vital aspect of European colonialism. It played a role in administrative, missionary, scientific, and commercial activities. As the Zimbabwean novelist Yvonne Vera put it, "The camera has often been a dire instrument. In Africa, as in most parts of the dispossessed, the camera arrives as part of the colonial paraphernalia, together with the gun and the bible."

But photography in colonialized societies was not *only* a dire instrument. Subject peoples often adopted photography for their own uses. There were, for instance, a number of studios in Lagos by the 1880s, where elites could go to pose for portraits. But such positive side effects aside, photography during colonial rule im-

aged the world in order to study, profit from, and own it. The
colonial gaze might describe as barbarous both the oba's beaded
crown and his regal right to conceal himself. This was one of the
repeated interactions between imperial powers and the popula-
tions they sought to control: the dominant power decided that
everything had to be seen and cataloged, a task for which photography was perfectly suited. Under the giant umbrella of colonialism, nothing would be allowed to remain hidden from the imperial authorities.

Imperialism and colonial photographic practices both flour-
ished in the nineteenth century, and both extended themselves,
with cosmetic adaptations, into the twentieth. In 1960, during
the horrific French war on Algeria, the French military assigned
a young soldier, Marc Garanger, to photograph people in an in-
ternment camp in the Kabylia region of northern Algeria. Thousands of people had been confined in the region under armed
guard, and the French military commander had decreed that ID
cards would be mandatory. As a picture of each prisoner was required, many of the local women were forced to remove their
veils. Women who did not wish to be seen were forced to sit for
photographs that were not for them. (Photography played a different, no less hostile, military role in the numerous aerial recon-
naissance missions by the French, which resulted in thousands of
negatives mapping the region.)

Garanger's photographs both record an injustice and occasion
it. His alternative, not an easy one, would have been to refuse the
order and go to prison. So, he sided with the oppressor. His pictures show us what we ought not to see: young and old women,
their hair free-flowing or plaited, one face after the other, by the
hundreds, collectively emanating refusal. The women of Kabylia
look through the photographer, certainly not considering him an

ally (no matter what he later tried to claim). Their gazes rise from the surface of the photograph, palpably furious. I know of few photographs harder to look at than these portraits of the quietly enraged women of Kabylia.

• • •

When we speak of "shooting" with a camera, we acknowledge the kinship of photography and violence. The anthropological photographs made in the nineteenth century under the aegis of colonial powers are related to the images created by contemporary photojournalists, including those who embed with military forces. Embedding is sometimes the only way to get a direct record, no matter how limited, of what is happening in an armed conflict. On occasion such an arrangement leads to images whose directness displeases the authorities, but a more common outcome has been that proximity to an army helps bolster the narrative preferred by the army, its selective perspective, its half-truths and outright falsehoods.

Still, photographic reportage has the power to quicken the conscience and motivate political commitments. Examples abound of photographs acting as catalysts in the public's understanding of vital issues, from the images of Bergen-Belsen in 1945 to the photograph of the Syrian toddler Alan Kurdi in 2015, which is credited with helping change German refugee policy. And yet, perhaps even more insistently, on a day-by-day, week-by-week basis, photography implicitly serves the powers that be. To insist that contemporary photographic practice, the making (and publishing) of images, generally serves the greater good is to misconstrue history, because it leaves out the question "Good for whom?" Such pictures aren't for their subjects any more than the photograph in Stone's book was for the Ijebus and their king.

Certain images underscore an unbridgeable gap and a never-to-be-toppled hierarchy. When a group of people is judged to be "foreign," it becomes far more likely that news organizations will run, for the consumption of their audiences, explicit, disturbing photographs of members of that group: starving children or bullet-riddled bodies. Meanwhile, the injury and degradation of those with whom readers perceive a kinship — a judgment often based on racial sympathy and class loyalties — is routinely treated in more circumspect fashion. This has hardly changed since critics and scholars first wrote about it, and it has hardly changed because the underlying political relationships between dominant and subject societies have hardly changed.

Without confronting this inequality, this misconstrual of history, photography will continue to describe itself as one thing (a force for liberation) while obdurately remaining another (an obedient appendage of state power). It will continue to be like the organs of the state that "spread democracy" and change regimes. Even when it appears to go against the state, it will do so only quaintly, beautifully, piteously, in terms that do not question the right of the state to assert power.

. . .

For how long will these radically unequal societal realities endure? Many affecting photographs have been made during the huge waves of international migration of the past few years. These pictures issue, as usual, from the presumed rights of photographers to depict the suffering of people "out there" for the viewing of those "back home." But in looking at these images — images of war, of starvation, of drowning people and exhausted caravans — we must go beyond the usual frames of pity and abjection.

When I look at the bewildering photographs of refugee camps

in Richard Mosse's 2018 book, *The Castle*, I do feel indicted. The imperial underpinnings of Mosse's project are inescapable: using military-grade thermal cameras, he makes extremely complex panoramic images (stitched together from hundreds of shots) of landscapes in the Middle East and Europe in which refugees have gathered or have been confined. His pictures echo the surveillance to which these bodies are already subjected. But the thermal imaging renders the images very dark, with the humans showing up as white shapes (almost like a negative). The picture conceals what it reveals. We see people but at the same time they remain hidden. This technique makes for uncanny images in which distressed people move about like the figures you see in dreams, indistinct but full of ghostly presence. At the Moria camp in Greece, it is snowing. We see a long snaking line of people, waiting. What are they waiting for? For some material handout, probably, for food or blankets or documents. But their waiting represents the deeper waiting of all those who have been confined in the antechamber of humanity. They are waiting to be allowed to be human.

Mosse's images, formally striking as they are, are unquestionably part of the language of visual domination. With his political freedom of movement and his expensive technical equipment, he makes meticulous pictures of suffering that end up in exquisite books and in art galleries. He is not the first photographer to aestheticize suffering, nor will he be the last. And yet, something breaks through. By suppressing color, by overwhelming the viewer with detail, by evoking racial horror rather than prettily displaying it and by including in his work philosophical considerations of the scenes he shows — *The Castle* contains essays by Judith Butler, Paul K. Saint-Amour, and Mosse himself, and a poem by Behrouz Boochani—he does something different from what most photojournalists do. He unsettles the viewer.

Photography's future will be much like its past. It will largely continue to illustrate, without condemning, how the powerful dominate the less powerful. It will bring the "news" and continue to support the idea that doing so—collecting the lives of others for the consumption of "us"—is a natural right. But I have a little bit of hope that an ethic of self-determination can be restored. I have hope that the refugees of Moria, Athens, Berlin, and Belgrade will gain a measure of privacy. The women of Kabylia will cover their faces and return to themselves as they wish to be. The oba's beaded crown will fall back into place, shadowing his face. Photography writes with light, but not everything wants to be displayed. Among the human rights is the right to remain obscure, unseen, and dark.

PART FOUR

COMING TO OUR SENSES

Experience

The river is at its river song. At this elevation, twelve hundred meters above sea level, the river is young and narrow, shallow and fast. Sunlight is filtered through the leaves of the trees on the riverbank, dappling the water's surface. The river is verged with midsummer grass, with large gray stones, some smooth, some jagged. He has picked his way down the bank and has settled on a large stone, either side of which is traversed by fast eddies. He is sensitive, sensate, sensible. *Sentire*: to feel, to perceive, to realize.

What's he sensing there, crouched forward, still as a stone in a flowing river, on that day, on the banks of the Valser Rhine? Perhaps he's as the figure described in Robert Lowell's "Waking Early Sunday Morning":

> . . . and now my body wakes
> to feel the unpolluted joy
> and criminal leisure of a boy —
> no rainbow smashing a dry fly
> in the white run is free as I,

here squatting like a dragon on
time's hoard before the day's begun!

That figure in the Valser Rhine is me. With my eyes I see the bright light on the water, with my ears hear the thrum and splash of the water, with my nose smell the grass and alpine flowers. I bring water to my mouth and I can taste its mineral intensity and the faint bouquet of summer grass. My fingers touch the stones rough and smooth, the bedlike grass, the marblelike pebbles, the fugitive water. And behind me, half buried in a hillside, is a mysterious building.

Christianity has often been terrified of the senses. It has tended to view them as portals for the Devil, and the easiest way to fall into sin. "The Desert of Religion," an illuminated manuscript made with ink and pigments on vellum around 1425 in northern England, uses the metaphor of a forest to describe the Christian's struggle. There are illustrations of the Tree of Faith, the Tree of Meekness, and the Tree of Spiritual Battles. On one striking page is a tree of the Five Senses. The trunk reads, "here growes a tree of leves fyne." The tree has five multifoliate leaves, each labeled with three text boxes: the first tells what sense organ is represented, the others, the kind of sin pertaining to that sense. One, for instance, reads, "of the eyes," followed by "unlawful" and "seeing": the sin of the eyes is unlawful seeing. The others have a similar structure: "of the ears, unlawful hearing," "of the nose, unlawful smelling," "of feet and hands, unlawful touching," "of the mouth, unlawful tasting."

With the passing of the centuries, European skepticism toward the senses did not quite go away. During the Dutch Golden Age, the morally unlawful acquired quite a bit of elegance. The vanitas still-life paintings of the seventeenth century were as much warnings about the fragility of life as they were indulgent exercises in the painterly evocation of surfaces, textures, and pleasures of every kind. They were full of things to taste, touch, smell, look at, and listen to. A painting such as Pieter Claesz's *Allegory of the Five Senses* is a ravishingly painted assemblage. There's the violin for hearing, the glowing coals and snuff box for smell, the wine glass for taste, the lamp for vision, and a variety of textures, of wood, glass, paper, and cloth, for touch. How precious is this cascade of senses. "Bless thy five wits," as Tom o' Bedlam says to Lear out on the heath. Bless your five senses.

Sense one: sight. Waking up one morning in early 2011, I was unable to see out of my left eye. This medical emergency astonished me into a new vulnerability. But I was fortunate: within days my vision came back. For years afterward, I explored the highways and byways of my relationship with my sense of sight, which culminated in a book of photographs and texts called *Blind Spot*, for which I found intertextual help from the Hebrew Bible, from Homer, and beyond.

Sense two: hearing. We ought to think not only of music but of the sheer possibilities inherent in acoustic sensitivity, from military infrasound to the subtle murmurations of the inner self gathered up by a stethoscope. Not that our way of hearing is the only way of hearing. Bats, for instance, have a sound world very far from ours, as Thomas Nagel sharply delineated in "What Is it Like to Be a Bat?," his famous thought experiment on consciousness. Nagel's work reminds me of a superb poem, "Bats' Ultrasound," by Les Murray. Murray, who was perhaps the most notable of all Australian poets, wrote brilliantly about animal life. I don't imagine that his poem, published in 1986, is necessarily in direct response to Nagel's belief that a bat's consciousness is not accessible to humans. But, somehow, "Bats' Ultrasound," in three quintains plus a final line, is as good a riposte to Nagel's assertion of untranslatability as any I know:

> Sleeping-bagged in a duplex wing
> with fleas, in rock-cleft or building
> radar bats are darkness in miniature,
> their whole face one tufty crinkled ear
> with weak eyes, fine teeth bared to sing.
>
> Few are vampires. None flit through the mirror.
> Where they flutter at evening's a queer
> tonal hunting zone above highest C.
> Insect prey at the peak of our hearing
> drone re to their detailing tee:
>
> *ah, eyrie-ire; aero hour, eh?*
> *O'er our ur-area (our era aye*
> *ere your raw row) we air our array*
> *err, yaw, row wry — aura our orrery,*
> *our eerie ü our ray, our arrow.*
>
> *A rare ear, our aery Yahweh.*

Sense three: taste. It is a rather mysterious one, an insulted sense, thought since ancient times to be intellectually inferior to sight and hearing, which are taken to have the capacity for disinterest. Taste is thought of as too vulnerable to pleasure, and therefore suspect. It is, as Giorgio Agamben writes, "a knowledge that cannot account for its judgments but, rather, enjoys them." Rousseau was getting at the same thing, or something similar, with his distinction between, on the one hand, "intellectual and moral impressions which we receive by way of the senses, but of which the senses are only the occasional causes," and on the other, "purely sensual impressions." In that former category, Rousseau puts colors and sounds. But taste is just taste, a pure sensuality: it does not, and cannot, signify.

Sense four: smell. We are acutely aware that this is the one in which humans are most radically inferior to other animals. Compared to dogs, elephants, or sharks, with their extraordinarily keen noses, we humans are paltry sniffers. A bear can smell a carcass twenty miles away. At a dozen yards or fewer, we can barely smell the jasmine fragrance someone else is wearing. We'd never make it in the wild.

Sense five: touch. Imagine the gesture of touching one's lips with one's finger, or touching a finger with one's lips, a gesture close to but not identical to kissing your finger. Musing on this gesture, Michel Serres delivers a marvelous phrase: "the I vibrates alternately on both sides of the contact." Serres is right. I am my finger, and I am my lips, and I am in both of these places imbued with intentionality. Touch is the reflexive sense. To touch is to be touched. To touch oneself is to be touched by oneself, to create a circle of which one is both the center and the circumference.

・・・

There are at least two wrinkles in this account of the senses. One is that there are more than five senses. We have always intuited this, but in modern times we have begun to codify senses beyond the traditional five in the Western tradition. I don't mean what people think of when they say the "sixth sense": not the paranormal. I mean the utterly normal, the physical, the actual that has merely been unsystematized. Though we no longer believe that there are only four elements, if you ask someone how many physical senses they have, they are likely still to answer, "Five." There are many more than that. There are nine, perhaps, or twenty-one. It depends on how you count, on how you categorize receptors. The original five are themselves *now* understood to be based on the fact that each has its own neural organization, and not simply on the fact of a visible sense organ. And on this basis, on the basis of neural organization, additional senses can be described.

The sense of pain, nociception, is neurologically distinct from the sense of touch, though much of its mechanism is also present on the skin. The ability to know where the different parts of your body are is proprioception: even with your eyes closed, you know exactly where your fingertips are at any given moment, and they needn't be touching anything for you to know that. Your sense of balance, equilibrioception, is dependent on your sense of sight, on the vestibular canals of your inner ear, and on your proprioception. We all have that essential and life-preserving sense of hot and cold called thermoception, with one set of receptors for heat detection and another set for cold detection. There are cutaneous thermoreceptors, on the skin, and there are homeostatic ones, which help the body regulate its internal temperature. That brings us up to nine. And there's the sense of time, the sense of gravity, even the very faint sense of where on the planet you are. The count expands. It's subtleties all the way down.

. . .

"And now my body wakes / to feel the unpolluted joy . . ."

You leave the river and approach the mysterious building like you are in a dream, a dream of approaching your own body, or waking from a dream to discover your own body anew, to discover that the building is a body, or to discover the idea of a body in the form of a building. Not a body's shape, nor its functions —

nothing so crude—but rather an experience mediated through architecture. The building presents you with a set of experiences that embody the sensitivities and the sensitive affordances of a body. It is as though the body had been reduced to its senses alone, and those senses had imagined themselves in the form of a building that could act on the body and draw out all its sensitivities. You approach the building in darkness, a long dark passage, a kind of descent, a hush, a calming of the body for what is to come. A turnstile, a passage, the changing room of dark burnished red wood enclosed in heavy black leather drapes. Beyond the drapes, you can begin to make out distant, muffled voices.

Then you walk down long steps, which ritualistically lower you into what seems an enormous grotto. But this is neither a grotto nor any other natural cavern: things are at right angles. You are aware of your bare feet on irregular stone, the wet and evanescent footprints of other bathers, their near-phantom bodies, the impression of their thrown voices in various languages echoing and fading in the darkness, the heavy mass of the building shot through with lighting as though the roof were fissured. Finally, you are immersed in the indoor pool, which is warm and blue.

• • •

The Therme is in the village of Vals, in the alpine Canton of Graubünden, in eastern Switzerland. Its architect is Peter Zumthor, and the building was completed in 1996 on the site of an ancient thermal spring. The building is new, but its aura is of something very old: Roman, pre-Roman, a realm of water, stone, darkness, ritual. As Mircea Eliade wrote, "Immersion in water signifies regression to the preformal, reincorporation into the undifferentiated mode of pre-existence." I have never been so in tune with my own body as in this cavern, with its cantilevered roofs, its massive stone floors, the dripping water, the enormous pillars of gneiss, the shimmering combined with the solidity. Never so in tune with my own body and never so released from it.

Inside the Therme, one experiences visceral simplicity and stark binaries: darkness and light, clarity and indistinctness, expansive height and the enclosure of small spaces. All is built of local gneiss, which glints with mica, feldspar, quartzite. It is bluish, grayish, greenish, stacked in precise slabs, cumulatively monumental. Where the water has been allowed to drip, there is a patina of iron, carbonates, sulfates. Around the perimeter of the indoor pool, off a passageway, are portals that invite entry. One seems to glow red at the entrance. You enter and descend into a pool at 107 degrees Fahrenheit, which is almost as hot as you can bear. This is the Fire Bath. Your body adjusts to it, and you emerge. Opposite is another portal, into a smaller room, its walls concrete and painted blue. This is the Ice Bath, at 57 degrees, which can only be endured for seconds. Further along is the entry into a warm pool full of small marigold petals and the misted fragrance of lavender, heaven on earth for the bather's olfactory bulb.

· · ·

The history of bathing is mythic. Diana and Actaeon, Susanna and the Elders, David and Bathsheba, Moses, Achilles. This is a realm of half-buried feelings. "The condensation of emotion," as Zumthor puts it. At the sweat stone, I encounter extreme humidity and the fragrance of eucalyptus. At the drinking stone, pure Valser water courses down my throat. In the sound room, which is square and high-ceilinged, with an entrance allowing only one person at a time, deep here in the heart of the continent, neck deep in water, lit from below, all alone and almost hypnotized, I begin to sing, and whatever I sing sounds strange and prehistoric.

It is a room designed for echo. One voice magically becomes a choir, the overtones creating unimagined resonances. The stone is a womb, the water amniotic.

. . .

I wrote earlier that there were at least two wrinkles in the account I had given of the senses. The second was already seeping into my description of the Therme, as light seeps into that building, and it is this: our senses are not isolated. In fact, they are often blended. The strongest cases of sense blending are described as joined or coupled sensation: synesthesia. People who are synesthetic experience the coupling of senses in highly individual and specific ways. Someone might consistently experience the musical pitch of B-flat as smelling of roses, or the letter F as sounding green. Modern neurology has been able to show that synesthesia, while highly idiosyncratic, is genetic. The genes responsible, of which there are several, are present in one in every twenty-three people. Synesthesia works in one direction, as a rule; for a given person, a sound induces a color, and not the other way around. The pairings tend to be consistent for a given person, but they differ from person to person. Also, what is being blended are not strictly the senses themselves, but modalities of sensing, such as colors, letters, shapes, and flavors (color associations are the most common type of synesthesia). A visual modality can blend with another visual modality.

In 1848, an eight-year-old named Ellen Emerson was attested as being synesthetic. She was the first documented synesthete in the United States, the first documented child synesthete anywhere, and also the first documented female synesthete. The evidence is in a letter written by a friend of her father's, who was helping care for Ellen and her siblings. "I was struck by Ellen's asking me, yesterday, while I was talking to Mrs. Brown, if I did not use 'colored words.' She said that she could tell the color of a great many words, and amused the children at school by doing so." Ellen Emerson was the daughter of Ralph Waldo Emerson. The family friend who wrote the letter to Ellen's father was Henry David Thoreau.

The synesthesia of Vladimir Nabokov is a vertiginously elaborate version of Ellen Emerson's "colored words." In *Speak, Memory*, his 1951 autobiography, he gives an account of just how precise was his identification of lexical sounds with specific colors:

> The long *a* of the English . . . has for me the tint of weathered wood, but a French *a* evokes polished ebony. This black group also includes hard *g* (vulcanized rubber) and *r* (a sooty rag being ripped). Oatmeal *n*, noodle-limp *l*, and the ivory-backed hand mirror of *o* take care of the whites. I am puzzled by my French *on* which I see as the brimming tension-surface of alcohol in a small glass. Passing on to the blue group, there is steely *x*, thundercloud *z*, and huckleberry *k*. Since a subtle interaction exists between sound and shape, I see *q* as browner than *k*, while *s* is not the light blue of *c*, but a curious mixture of azure and mother-of-pearl.

It's extraordinary, and goes on in this vein for quite a while, all the way to *v*, which Nabokov triumphantly declares he has finally perfectly matched with the entry for Rose Quartz in Maerz and Paul's *Dictionary of Color*.

Only Nabokov is Nabokov, but the scientific study of synesthesia has in itself been valuable because it sheds light on a general sophistication in how we all interact with our sense modalities. I don't believe that I am synesthetic, but I cannot always account for the intensity of my sensations, and I have experienced some interaction of numbers and colors: three is red, seven is green. Four red roses would make me feel uncomfortable, since roses are red and want to be three or five. But these are faint associations for me, and we are all associative to one degree or the other. I was surprised but not surprised one afternoon when my mother looked at a mug with a distinctively shaped handle and said a single word: "Obama." I immediately understood her: the mug's "ear" was just like his. Just like his, but some sort of associative leap had to be made.

. . .

There's a non-arbitrary mapping of sound to shape—present in about 90 percent of the general population—called the "kiki and bouba effect." It was described by Wolfgang Köhler in 1929. Köhler's experiment, conducted on the island of Tenerife, asked people to match bulbous or spiky shapes to the words "takete" and "baluba." In 2001, researchers Ramachandran and Hubbard repeated the experiment with American college students and with Tamil speakers in India, using the words "kiki" and "bouba." The "correct" matches—matching kiki with the spiky shape and bouba with the rounded one—were made by more than 95 percent of the subjects. What the kiki (or takete) and bouba (or balouba) effect suggests is that the naming of objects is not random. The rounded shape your mouth makes pushes "bouba" toward roundness, while the wide angularity of the mouth in saying "kiki," as well as the shortness of the *ih* sound, help associate it with a spiky shape. The cross-sensory effect of bouba and kiki shows up in musical sounds, where a pinging sound is assigned "kiki" and a boomy one is "bouba," and in tastes, where a tart taste is "kiki" and a creamy one is "bouba."

We are all highly mingled within ourselves. Most of us are exquisitely suggestible under the influence of certain cues, always one petite shell-shaped madeleine away from a spiral of memory. In 1887, the American chemist Charles Henry Piesse published *Olfactics and the Physical Senses*. In that book, we find an account of a peculiar speculation by Piesse's father, Septimus Piesse. The elder Piesse proposed a taxonomy he called "the Gamut of Odors." He proposed the primary odors to be Camphor, Lemon, Jasmine, Rose, Almond, Clove, and Santal. Going further, he assigned each to a musical note, and also assigned notes to a range of non-primary odors, from the high F of civet, to the low C of patchouli. Middle C is jasmine. The smells are arranged in a musical scale the elder Piesse called an "odophone." To his credit, the younger Piesse does not definitively declare whether he believes or disbelieves his father's speculations.

Piesse's assignation of jasmine to middle C reminds me of an incident from many years ago when I went hiking in the Jawara Hills, outside the city of Jos in northern Nigeria. It was a day of unforgettable beauty and clarity: the pure air of the hills, our discovery of a milky blue lake, the sheer white cliff setting off one side of it. Near the end of the hike, hours after we last ran into anyone, we came upon a jasmine bush, abundant with white bloom. I plucked a bunch of florets and, bruising the petals with my fingers, brought them to my nose. And at the very moment I did so, at the very instant I received the olfactory sensation of concentrated jasmine in pure mountain air, a cloud of white butterflies rose from the bush. I thought I was hallucinating or having a stroke. But it was just pure narrative coincidence. Ever since then, whenever I smell jasmine, I see white butterflies.

Charles Dickens, in *Household Words*, makes the following spooky claim:

Is jasmine, then, the mystical Meru—the center, the Delphi, the Omphalos of the floral world? Is it the point of departure, the one unapproachable and indivisible unit of fragrance? Is jasmine the Isis of flowers, with veiled face and covered feet, to be loved of all yet discovered by none? Beautiful jasmine! If it be so, the rose ought to be dethroned, and the Inimitable enthroned queen in her stead. Revolutions and abdications are exciting sports; suppose we create a civil war among the gardens, and crown the jasmine empress and queen of all.

. . .

In March 1994, Alfred Kazin wrote the following: "My heart sank when I heard that Bellow once said, 'Who is the Tolstoy of the Zulus? The Proust of the Papuans? I'd be glad to read him.'" Bellow's statement was not completely surprising; his pronouncements had taken a conservative turn a number of years before that. It did, however, add a hectic few weeks to the American culture wars of the mid-1990s, as both defenders and detractors spoke out. Bellow took to the pages of the *New York Times* with an essay in his own defense. Reading it now, one can still note his pique steaming off the page. He slashes in all directions, taking a different turn in almost every successive paragraph.

First, Bellow says that he is only *alleged* to have said any such thing. Then he says he certainly said it nowhere in print. Then he says, "The scandal is entirely journalistic in origin, the result of a misunderstanding." Then he seems to concede that he did say it, in some form, but that it was in order to make a distinction between literate and preliterate societies. By the next paragraph, he says his remarks were "off the cuff obviously." And then he argues that since neither the Bulgarians nor the Americans have a Proust, they should be offended too. Of course, he did not

say anything about Americans or Bulgarians in the original statement—the reason being (to quote the argument he makes in a
later paragraph) that we have to "make allowance for what we
outsiders cannot hope to fathom in another society." Americans
and Bulgarians are not foreign to this conception of the world, as
he imagines Zulus or Papuans to be.

In the short space of his opinion piece, one incensed justifi-
cation follows another: people no longer have a sense of humor,
rage is prestigious, Black child gangsters are killing people for saying the wrong thing. Nowhere in this rant is there any notion that
the Zulu or the Papuan might have a right of response, or even be
able to recognize the layers of condescension involved. They are
simply too primitive to be imaginable inside this argument, other
than as the material of argumentation. Never mind that there are
actual Zulu and Papuan novelists. B. W. Vilakazi, Vincent Eri,
and others are made to disappear. Finally, coming to the end of
his screed, Bellow decides that anyone who criticizes him is the
equivalent of an anti-Semite or Stalinist, and that his right to dis-
cuss a "major public question" is being infringed. He concludes:
"We can't open our mouths without being denounced as racists,
misogynists, supremacists, imperialists, or fascists." This phrasing
is unfortunately familiar now, and its actual meaning is usually as
follows: "We can't say racist, misogynist, supremacist, imperial-
ist, or fascist things without having them recognized as such."

I've long wondered what an adequate riposte to Bellow's rage
would be. One response I like very much was formulated by the
late writer Ralph Wiley, and quoted in Ta-Nehisi Coates's *Between the World and Me*. Wiley said, "Tolstoy is the Tolstoy of the
Zulus, unless you find profit in fencing off universal properties of
mankind into exclusive tribal ownership." I love that response because it identifies accurately how we live: in a polyphony of cul-

tural influence that is not eclipsed by the other facts of race, age, gender, citizenship, or historical period, an individuated experience of the world that takes us from Li Po to Zadie Smith and all stops in between. We live in each other's worlds, worlds in which our Tolstoy is Tolstoy, no matter where we might be.

I propose a second response to Bellow, in the form of a speculative narrative. Imagine an evening late in the year 1385. The ooni, or king, of Ife holds a consultation over, say, a land dispute. The ooni is seated on his throne in the shadowy inner room of the palace, arrayed in magnificent flowing white robes, which signify his purity and his association with the god Obatala. This ooni is named Obalufon II and he is the third king to ascend the throne of Ife. He had been crowned, then in a terrible succession dispute, deposed by his uncle Oranmiyan. But the struggle continued, and eventually Oranmiyan had been overthrown and Obalufon II returned to power.

By 1385, he is older, wiser. The city-state of Ife, 135 miles north of West Africa's Atlantic Coast, has been secured. On the king's face is a serene prosperity. He has the cheeks of a man who laughs. But he is not laughing, only smiling, mysteriously. Were we able to properly see Obalufon's dark-complected face — in this story that I am imagining — were it not obscured by the beaded crown, which scatters light across his face, we would see his calmness and ingenuity. We would see the natural set of his lips, the line of that enigmatic smile, the flare of the nostrils. All this fine detail we must imagine, but still, we can see behind the shifting beads in the darkened room that it is him. Aspects of his physiognomy come across unmistakably.

Obalufon II leans over to an advisor and whispers his judgment. The king is second only to the gods, and his voice is not to be heard trivially. The advisor speaks out, rendering his verdict on the matter at hand: where the demarcations of land are to be set, to whom restitution must be paid, what the penalties are against anyone who contravenes the royal decision. Given the variables at play, given the various feelings of the various parties involved, his Majesty has spoken wisely. Jurisprudence always contains an element of guesswork in any case, and wisdom is guaranteed to displease at least some claimants. In a hundred years, as with so many things in human affairs, this particular decision won't matter much, won't matter at all. There will be other conflicts, other contests, and only faint memories, if any memories at all, of this evening. In six hundred years, kings will almost be irrelevant.

But I return to this imaginary moment, and close in on the point: only a few of those gathered in court, sworn to secrecy, know that this man is not actually the king, Obalufon II. It is someone else, pretending to be him: a high chief wearing a hyper-realistic mask (plate 6). Obalufon II himself has been dead for years. The mask is now in his place. It is made of almost pure copper, an expensive material, difficult to cast. At this same moment, the technology for lost-wax casting of copper is lost to Europe, and will only be revived in the time of Donatello. The Obalufon mask is made to the precise size of the dead king's face, and when it is worn, it extends his beneficial rule. In a few months, the sacred subterfuge will be over. The next king, the fourth ooni of Ife, will ascend the throne. Obalufon will be deified and become the god of sculptors, and one of the most honored of Ife's kings.

But for now, on this evening in 1385, we are still suspended in a necessary deception. The ooni rises, leaves the room, and the people of Ife fall and bow in piety. His white robes cloud him in the half-darkness, and the air is full of his special music, the music of Obatala: an ensemble of *igbin* drums, with their slack and deep sound, accompanied by the chatter of metal percussion. The eyes

of onlookers see the carved wooden posts of the palace, the scintillating robes, the brass sculptures representing the ancestors and
royal families, and the mask, which is the face of the king, which
is the signal of tradition, which is the guarantee of personhood.
Their ears receive and navigate the polyrhythmic percussion, the
sounds in high and low registers, finely discriminating between
the instrumental timbres. Their noses smell the sweet censers
and ritual smoke of *turari* that fill the court. Their tongues are bitter with the taste of ceremonial kola nut, which is distributed to
stimulate wisdom and focus. Their hands and feet are in contact
with woven mats and the fine red earth. Their skin feels the heat
of the room, and their bodies locate them in the pulsing crowd,
never too far from or too close to their fellow courtiers. There is
a sense of time, but not as governed by clocks. All their anten-
nae are tuned in, all their receptors activated—they are actively
proprioceptive, noniceptive, thermoceptive, equilibrioceptive—
all their habit and memories help situate them inside the flux of
existence, in their proper places in the lineage of the living, the
dead, and the unborn. They are at this very moment collectively
human because they are sensible in every sense of the word. There
can be no condescension toward the thickness of their sense experiences. And we, as sensing beings, sense it all with the participants of this long-ago West African court. Our senses, like theirs,
are like a river at its river song, like a piano struck at middle C, like
a sudden whiff of jasmine, like that unsought, irrevocable, unforgettable, ineffable cloud of white butterflies.

Epiphany

"Presently, I, too, went down one of the side streets, an even smaller and more congested one, along which prewar buildings jostled vertiginously, each with an elaborate fire escape that it offered like a transparent mask to the world."

In the second half of *Open City*, Julius gets the news that his beloved professor has died. This news induces him to walk a great distance, from Harlem down to Chinatown. It is a somewhat complicated passage, of which this is the opening. The pages that follow that opening were my attempt at a certain kind of dense, epiphanic, city writing, which I relate to a number of literary and filmic forebears.

The idea of epiphany summons two thoughts, generally. One is religious: the sudden and overwhelming appearance of the Divine into everyday life, as experienced, for instance, by Julian of Norwich, Teresa of Avila, and many holy figures through the ages. The other is literary. Epiphany is now perhaps as strongly, or even more strongly, connected to a certain idea expressed in European modernism, and emphasized in its aftermath. The idea is especially prominent in Joyce's two early prose works, *Dubliners* —

which includes "The Dead" — and *Portrait of the Artist as a Young Man*. Epiphany, as understood by Joyce, and practiced thereafter, has to do with heightened sensation and flashes of insight, often of the kind that helps a character solve a problem. This is the definition he gave the term, in an early version of *Portrait of the Artist as a Young Man*: "a sudden spiritual manifestation."

"The Dead" begins at an annual Christmas gathering for friends and family in Dublin early in the twentieth century. After the party, we are with a couple, the Conroys, heading to their hotel. And then we are with just the troubled thoughts of Gabriel Conroy, who is ruminating on what his wife Gretta has just told him about something in her deep past: when she was a girl, she loved a boy and the boy loved her. This boy, Michael Furey, waiting outside her window all those years ago like a figure in myth, or like a figure in a faintly remembered dream, later caught some illness and died. A song she heard at the party earlier that night had brought all this back to her. And now she is asleep in the hotel room and her husband, Gabriel, is awake, with *his* blizzard of emotions.

A few light taps upon the pane made him turn to the window. It had begun to snow again. He watched sleepily the flakes, silver and dark, falling obliquely against the lamplight. The time had come for him to set out on his journey westward. Yes, the newspapers were right: snow was general all over Ireland. It was falling on every part of the dark central plain, on the treeless hills, falling softly upon the Bog of Allen and, farther westward, softly falling into the dark mutinous Shannon waves. It was falling, too, upon every part of the lonely churchyard on the hill where Michael Furey lay buried. It lay thickly drifted on the crooked crosses and headstones, on the spears of the little gate, on the barren thorns. His soul swooned slowly as he heard the snow falling faintly through the universe and faintly falling, like the descent of their last end, upon all the living and the dead.

So, having zoomed in on the smallness of Gabriel Conroy's concerns, of his angst at not having known the long-guarded secrets of his wife's heart, Joyce zooms out again, taking in the entire landscape, deploying chiasmus and alliteration, the snow "falling softly" and "softly falling" and "falling faintly" and "faintly falling" on all the living and the dead.

It is as classic as a twentieth-century literary passage gets. I cited "The Dead" directly in *Open City*, a book that is about many things, but certainly about how one man's life is invaded by literature and literary antecedents. My narrator, Julius, is in Brussels, looking for his grandmother. He has spent most of his time wandering around in a haze of depression. To him, Belgian history and current Belgian politics both feel like open wounds, but there are personal pains he's intent on suppressing too. But he's also had a series of random encounters in the city that now come back to him. His journey is coming to an end. In one paragraph, I substitute rain for snow, and Belgium for Ireland, but otherwise make few changes to Joyce's original. The lifting is obvious and unsubtle. Mature poets, as Eliot had it, steal (it is obviously another matter if your intention is to never be found out). My literary interests have been shaped in part by modernism, by Joyce and Woolf, by Mann, Musil, Broch: the flow of thoughts through minds, the blending of sensation into lyric passages. Far from having any anxiety of influence, I am skeptical of an originality that does not place itself in conversation with antecedents.

The ending of "The Dead" showed up again in a later book of

mine, *Blind Spot.* The passage, titled "Rivaz," is an account of a walk, and it is the penultimate entry in the book. It is a hymn of gratitude, full of sunshine, not nocturnal, far from rain and snow, the Joycean rush of it becoming apparent only at the very end.

> I rest at a concrete outcrop with a bunting of vintners' blue nets, a blue the same color as the lake. It is as though something long awaited has come to fruition. A gust of wind sweeps in from across the lake. The curtain shifts, and suddenly everything can be seen. The scales fall from our eyes. The landscape opens. No longer are we alone: they are with us now, have been all along, all our living and all our dead.

What we think of as the Joycean epiphany has strong nineteenth-century models — in Emerson, in Wordsworth — and it has had a vigorous afterlife in twentieth-century fiction. Perhaps too vigorous, if you are Charles Baxter, author of "Against Epiphanies." Baxter sees too many pat epiphanies, too many neat flashes of insight and pithy summations in contemporary American fiction, particularly in short stories. The lyric moment happens, and the conundrum the character has been mulling is suddenly solved. It's all too easy. I think Baxter's right, and I take advantage of the flexibility of the term epiphany to think not about this particular narrow narrative device, but rather of a stylistic mode which, as often as not, puts us in place but neither advances the plot nor solves any problem.

This passage from *Mrs. Dalloway,* for instance, does not really bring some staggering moment of insight. What it does is cook a list, nourish the eye and the ear, and bring us closer to Clarissa's consciousness and to ours:

For Heaven only knows why one loves it so, how one sees it so, making it up, building it around one, tumbling it, creating it every moment afresh; but the veriest frumps, the most dejected of miseries sitting on doorsteps (drink their downfall) do the same; can't be dealt with, she felt positive, by Acts of Parliament for that very reason: they love life. In people's eyes, in the swing, tramp, and trudge; in the bellow and the uproar; the carriages, motor cars, omnibuses, vans, sandwich men shuffling and swinging; brass bands; barrel organs; in the triumph and the jingle and the strange high singing of some aeroplane overhead was what she loved; life; London; this moment in June.

Reading Woolf, we are with her: creating every moment afresh, awakened further with each semicolon. A different master of this mode is W. G. Sebald, who, of the writers I have studied, might be the one in whom this intense, emotionally charged but intellectually unflagging approach is most pervasive. Sebald wrote entire books that are almost nothing but the headiness of an associative dream. *The Rings of Saturn* is a narrative of a fictional walk in Suffolk, the journal of a man who seems to carry around an antiquarian hypertext library in his head. I'm especially taken with the skill with which Sebald, at book length, connects one thought to another. If you stare hard, you can see the stitching—he'll say "it occurs to me that," or that so-so "may well have had an eye for these things"—but you only see it if you're searching. Otherwise, what you have is a highly controlled delivery, a billowing cloud seen in slow motion. Here is how *The Rings of Saturn* ends:

Maundy Thursday, the 13th of April 1995, was also the day on which Clara's father, shortly after being taken to hospital in Coburg, departed this life. Now, as I write, and think once more of our history, which is but a long account of calamities, it occurs to me that at one time the only acceptable expression of profound grief, for ladies of the upper classes, was to wear heavy robes of black silk taffeta or black crêpe de chine. Thus at Queen Victoria's funeral, for example, the Duchess of Teck allegedly made her appearance in what contemporary fashion magazines described as a breathtaking gown with billowing veils, all of black Mantua silk of which the Norwich silk weavers Willett & Nephew, just before the firm closed down for good, had created, uniquely for this occasion, and in order to demonstrate their unsurpassed skills in the manufacture of mourning silks, a length of some sixty paces. And Sir Thomas Browne, who was the son of a silk merchant and may well have had an eye for these things, remarks in a passage of the *Pseudodoxia Epidemica* that I can no longer find that in the Holland of his time it was customary, in a home where there had been a death, to drape black mourning ribbons over all the mirrors and canvases depicting landscapes or people or the fruits of the field, so that the soul, as it left the body, would not be distracted on its final journey, either by a reflection of itself or by a last glimpse of the land now being lost forever.

I still remember my shock when I read *The Rings of Saturn* for the first time, a shock of illumination that was also a shock of recognition. The literary attitude I'm describing is characterized by a certain density, whether it is dealing with a dark and melancholy interiority, as in Sebald, or with the thrum and possibility of city life, as in Woolf, Walter Benjamin, or Bruno Schulz. Cities are made of multiplicity, and they invite inventory. To list is, somehow, to love. The following is from Toni Morrison's *Jazz*, a book whose acceleration, attack, and improvisatory slyness honor the music of its title:

Breathing hurts in weather that cold, but whatever the problems of being winterbound in the City they put up with them because it is worth anything to be on Lenox Avenue safe from fays and the things they think up; where the sidewalks, snow-covered or not, are wider than the main roads of the towns where they were born and perfectly ordinary people can stand at the stop, get on the streetcar, give the man the nickel, and ride anywhere you please, although you don't please to go many places because everything you want is right where you are: the church, the store, the party, the women, the men, the postbox (but no high schools), the furniture store, street newspaper vendors, the bootleg houses (but no banks), the beauty parlors, the barbershops, the juke joints, the ice wagons, the rag collectors, the pool halls, the open food markets, the number runner, and every club, organization, group, order, union, society, brotherhood, sisterhood or association imaginable.

"Everything you want is right where you are," she writes. The scene is like that concept of the novel Stendhal wrote of in *The Red and the Black*: "A mirror carried along a high road." We find a similar inventorial approach in Orhan Pamuk's *Istanbul*. The subject of this passage is *hüzün*, the melancholia specific to Istanbul and Turkish history itself:

I am speaking of the evenings when the sun sets early, of the fathers under the streetlamps in the back streets returning home carrying plastic bags. Of the old Bosphorus ferries moored to deserted stations in the middle of winter, where sleepy sailors scrub the decks, pail in hand and one eye on the black-and-white television in the distance; of the old booksellers who lurch from one financial crisis to the next and then wait shivering all day for a customer to appear; of the barbers who complain that men don't shave as much after an economic crisis; of the children who play ball between the cars on cobblestoned streets; of the covered women who stand at remote bus stops clutching plastic shopping bags and speak to no one as they wait for the bus that never arrives; of the empty boathouses of the old Bosphorus villas . . .

Pamuk takes it very far indeed, and this passage runs on, as a single sentence, for several pages, coming to more than a hundred lines. Here's how it ends:

. . . of every thing being broken, worn out, past its prime; of the storks flying south from the Balkans and northern and western Europe as autumn nears, gazing down over the entire city as they waft over the Bosphorus and the islands of the Sea of Marmara; of the crowds of men smoking cigarettes after the national soccer matches, which during my childhood never failed to end in abject defeat: I speak of them all.

Each prepositional phrase is set off with the device "of the" such and such—like a chain of biblical "begats"—and each recalls the opening "I am speaking of": of the evenings, of the fathers, of the old Bosphorus ferries, of the storks flying south. The repetition invites a hypnosis over the length of this gargantuan passage, and the technique is evocative of the fog of melancholy that the passage itself is describing, a hypnosis like that triggered by "falling"—the repeated word itself trochaic, *falling*—in Joyce's "The Dead."

And one cannot help but imagine, in this kind of inventory, an authorial and narrative self guiding us through the experience of city life, through its crowds and personages and ever shifting sights. At times it's as though such authors are obeying Isher-wood's dictum: "I am a camera with its shutter open, quite pas-sive, recording, not thinking."

In literature, the camera is metaphorical; in film, it is literal. Cabiria, the lovelorn sex worker who is the hero of Fellini's 1957 film *Nights of Cabiria*, is certainly not Federico Fellini. The role is played to perfection by Giulietta Masina. And yet, at certain heightened moments, what we experience is a merging of her vision with his, and that vision becomes ours as well. In the final scene of *Nights of Cabiria*, Cabiria, disappointed in love yet again, wanders from the edge of a desolate lake into the quiet woods. She's all alone, she's been crying and now wears a stony expres-sion. Music begins to play, she walks past trees and is now on a road. First one woman enters the scene, then another, lively, call-ing out, then several characters in the distance, prancing, play-ing music. Guitars, party hats, a motorcycle, an accordion, all be-come visible onscreen. The screen fills up with youthful revelers. Cabiria continues walking down the road, but the night's temper has changed. The music gets louder, the revelers try to draw her into their revelry. "Buona sera," one sweet-voiced girl says, and poor sad-faced Cabiria, with the makeup of a circus clown, softly smiles. The music builds to a crescendo and she's smiling more broadly now, through tears.

8½, made later, is a film about making a film. The conclusion to *8½* is like a perfected form of the idea Fellini had first attempted six years earlier in *Nights of Cabiria*. It is a longer scene, it is more complicated, but the same energy pertains: that of an individual swept up in the sights and sounds and personae of others all around, all that activity rising to a crescendo, a sensational cre-scendo, because all the senses are being excited. We see things, we hear the voices and the music, and we imagine all the things the characters must be feeling. Guido, the lead, played by Marcello Mastroianni, is experiencing all the complexities of his life as a dream sequence in the form of a grand parade—his long-dead parents, his colleagues, his lovers, everyone is magically there—with himself as the band leader.

Fellini's filmmaking, Nino Rota's music, infectious joy. More sober is James Salter in his memoir *Burning the Days*. This passage from Salter is one to which I say, yes, this, too, is where I want to be. We are brought across the landscape by a solitary figure on whom all of it, out there, is having an effect, who is receiving all of it with senses tuned. It is morning, but light is still low. If it had music, it would be an andante, the music of flight and morning:

> Below, the earth has shed its darkness. There is the silver of count-less lakes and streams. The greatest things to be seen, the ancients wrote, are sun, stars, water, and clouds. Here among them, of what is one thinking? I cannot remember but probably of noth-ing, of flying itself, the imperishability of it, the brilliance. You do not think about the fish in the great winding river, thin as string, miles below, or the frogs in the glinting ponds, or they of you; they know little of you, though once, just after takeoff, I saw the shadow of my plane skimming the dry grass like the wings of god and passing over, frozen by the noise, a hare two hundred feet below. That lone hare, I, the morning sun, and all that lay beyond it were for an instant joined, like an eclipse.

I am dazzled and helped by passages of this kind. Conversa-tions between characters are all well and good; countesses must, I suppose, sweep into rooms, as they do in certain novels. But the secret reason I read, the only reason I read, is precisely for those moments in which the story being told is deeply alert to the world, an alertness that sees things as they are or dreams things as they could be. Those moments that are like a dark forest, a wide sky, an unplumbable mystery, or, in Heaney's words, a "hurry through which known and strange things pass."

. . .

For years now, I have also been thinking of "Naples" by Benjamin and Lacis, Rilke's *The Notebooks of Malte Laurids Brigge*, Marquez's *One Hundred Years of Solitude*, Hesse's *Siddhartha*, and Schulz's extraordinary and surreal *Street of Crocodiles*, these various texts of sensorial muchness. My memory is suddenly drawn back to Schulz's cinnamon shops in Drogobych between the wars, their dark and solemn interiors, the rare and dark goods they contained. He knew that inside shops we find inventories no less rich than those of cities.

Fellini's medium is so different from mine, and his mood is often antic, garrulous, and radically unlike what I try to do in my own writing. But I have had wonderful technical help from his films: *Nights of Cabiria, La Dolce Vita, 8½, Roma*. I understood better where the movement was in that final passage of "The Dead" — in a sense, what the camera movement was — or how its snow could become rain, by thinking of *Roma*. That film, which was made late in Fellini's career, and is about Rome, takes place largely on a soundstage at the Cinecittà studios. But the opening of the film and its ending are shot *al fresco* in the city of Rome. Near the opening, Fellini presents us with a long and mystifying sequence on the Grande Raccordo Anulare, the ring road surrounding the city. Like the Lagos in which I grew up, like São Paulo, like Chicago, Rome is a city of very complicated traffic. That traffic — its ongoingness, its tedium, its incessancy, but also its irrepressible variety of incident — is the true subject of Fellini's Dantesque opening sequence in *Roma*. The entire sequence is about nine minutes long. Darkness gradually falls before our very eyes, the scene stretches out, and we are immersed in a kind of theater of reality, like an image in reverse of Woolf's perfect day in June. There are fires, followed by wilder fires. There are firefighters. We see an overturned truck, dead livestock, more rain, protesters; deeper and deeper we go into the industrial sublime until it all comes to a traffic standstill, with a soundtrack of thunder and blaring car horns, the whole scene lit by frequent lightning, on a road next to the Colosseum.

Epiphany is not only revelation or insight, it is also the reassembly of the self through the senses. It is an engagement with the things that quicken the heart, through the faculties of the body, the things that catch the heart off guard and blow it open. Stendahl's mirror and Isherwood's camera are devices of receptivity and indiscriminate attention. They facilitate an overwhelming pileup of detail that shakes the sensible self to its core.

The passage from *Open City* that I signaled at the beginning of this essay was formed in the forge of these many influences. Julius begins at a loss for words, which he addresses by going for a walk. After walking for seven miles, he arrives in Chinatown. I quote the passage at length to make its flow and rhythm apparent:

> Presently, I, too, went down one of the side streets, an even smaller and more congested one, along which prewar buildings jostled vertiginously, each with an elaborate fire escape that it offered like a transparent mask to the world. Electric wires, wooden poles, abandoned buntings, and a thicket of signs clotted the façades all the way up to the tops of the four- and five-story buildings. The shop windows advertised dental products, tea, and herbs. Large bins were filled to the brim with gnarled ginger and

medicinal roots, and there was such a complete motley of goods and services that, after a while, to see a shop window full of hanging carcasses of roast duck succeeded by another one crammed with tailors' dummies, yet another full of fluttering printed leaflets in a half dozen sun-bleached variants of red, and that in its turn followed by a jumble of bronze and porcelain Buddha figures, came to seem a natural progression. Into this last shop, I entered, to escape the dizzying activity of the tiny street.

The shop, of which I was the sole customer, was a microcosm of Chinatown itself, with an endless array of curious objects: a profusion of bamboo cages as well as finely worked metal ones, hanging like lampshades from the ceiling; hand-carved chess sets on the ancient-looking bar between the customer and the shopkeeper's bay; imitation Ming Dynasty lacquerware, which ranged in size from tiny decorative pots to round-bellied vases large enough to conceal a man; humorous pamphlets of the "Confucius say" variety, which had been printed in English in Hong Kong and which gave advice to those gentlemen who wished to find success with women; fine wooden chopsticks set on porcelain chopstick stands; glass bowls of every hue, thickness, and design; and, in a seemingly endless glass-fronted gallery high above the regular shelves, a series of brightly painted masks that ran through every facial expression possible in the dramatist's art.

In the midst of this cornucopia sat an old woman, who, having looked up briefly when I came in, was now fully reabsorbed in her Chinese newspaper, preserving a hermetic air that, it was easy to believe, hadn't been disturbed since horses drank water from the troughs outside. Standing there in that quiet, mote-filled shop, with the ceiling fans creaking overhead, and the wood-paneled walls disclosing nothing of our century, I felt as if I had stumbled into a kink in time and place, that I could easily have been in any one of the many countries to which Chinese merchants had traveled and, for as long as trade had been global, set up their goods for sale. And, right away, as though to confirm this illusion, or at least to extend it, the old woman said something to me in Chinese and gestured outside. I saw a boy in a ceremonial uniform walk by with a bass drum. He was presently followed by a row of men with brass instruments, none of them playing, but all walking solemnly in step, marching down the narrow street, which seemed magically to have cleared itself of shoppers for their passage. The old woman and I watched them from the eerie calm of the shop, in which only the ceiling fans were audible, and row after row of these members of a Chinese marching band marched past, with their tubas, trombones, clarinets, trumpets: men of all ages, some with jowled faces, others looking as if they were just reaching puberty, with the first black traces of peach fuzz on their chins, but all with the most profound earnestness, carrying their golden instruments aloft, row after row, until, as if to bookend them, there marched past at the last a trio of snare drums and a final massive bass drum carried by an enormous man. I followed them with my eyes until the procession trickled beyond the last of the bronze Buddhas that sat looking outward from the shop's window. The Buddhas smiled at the scene with familiar serenity, and all the smiles seemed to me to be one smile, that of those who had stepped beyond human worries, the archaic smile that also played on the lips of the funeral steles of Greek kouroi, smiles that portended not pleasure but rather total detachment. From beyond the shop, the old lady and I heard the first series of notes from the trumpet, playing for two bars. Those twelve notes, spiritual cousins of the offstage clarion in Mahler's Second Symphony, were taken up by the entire band. It was a chromatic, blues-inflected figure that must have had its first life in a mission hymn, a dirge that was like a tempest heard from far away, or the growl of waves when the sea is out of sight. The song wasn't one I was able to identify but, in all respects, it matched the simple sincerity of songs I had last sung in the school yard of the Nigerian Military School, songs from the Anglican songbook *Songs of Praise*, which were for us a daily ritual, many years before and thousands of miles away from where I stood in that dusty, sun-suffused shop. I trembled as the throaty chorus of brass instruments spilled into that space, as the tuba ambled across the lower notes, and as the whole sound came into the shop like shafts of interrupted light. And then, with almost imperceptible slowness, the music began to fall in volume as the band marched farther and farther into the noise of the city.

Whether it expressed some civic pride or solemnized a funeral I could not tell, but so closely did the melody match my memory of those boyhood morning assemblies that I experienced the sudden disorientation and bliss of one who, in a stately old house and at a great distance from its mirrored wall, could clearly see the world doubled in on itself. I could no longer tell where the tangible universe ended and the reflected one began. This point-for-point imitation, of each porcelain vase, of each dull spot of shine on each stained teak chair, extended as far as where my reversed self had, as I had, halted itself in midturn. And this double of mine had, at that precise moment, begun to tussle with the same problem as its equally confused original. To be alive, it seemed to me, as I stood there in all kinds of sorrow, was to be both original and reflection, and to be dead was to be split off, to be reflection alone.

Writing is a bid for testimony as well as prophecy. It is a commitment shored up by history, by the parade, by memory, by music, by shops which are like cities and cities which are like shops, by solitude and by the collective, by what we have read and what we have remembered, by love and despair, by the living and the dead.

Ethics

When we speak of migration, it is easy to resort to watery language: we speak of a "flow" of refugees, an "influx," a "wave," a "flood." These are not neutral terms: they make the condition of our fellow human beings a cause for alarm, not on their behalf, but on ours. But people are not water, they are not inanimate. When I watch the clips of slave-trading from Libya—the clips that so reminded me of Caravaggio's terrifying late painting *The Beheading of Saint John the Baptist*—I am not watching a wave or a flood. I am watching people being sold. The numbers are called out, and I witness a human being un-humaned. Their abductors refer to them as "merchandise"; each is sold for the equivalent of a few hundred dollars. An obscenity that should not happen to anyone, an obscenity that should not be seen by anyone.

Humanity is on the move. As of 2019, there were some sixty-seven million people in one condition of migrancy or another. The numbers will only rise and will come to include some of us who don't expect to be included. Part of what draws me to Caravaggio is his imagination for the unhoused, the unhomed. His sympathy for those marginal conditions was shaped by his own experience. When I look at his tender, violent work, I see that experience transmuted into a work of witness. We tend to think of the news as a natural phenomenon, rather than one shaped by culture, privilege, and imperialism. With Caravaggio, I feel compelled to consider what it might mean to abandon the conventions of "raising awareness," of what it might mean to commit to the more dangerous work of bearing witness. The one who merely raises awareness can still pretend to neutrality, while the one who bears witness has already taken sides, has already committed to being unprofessional.

There is a difference between reading about something and hearing something, an irreducible difference between being told about something and seeing something. The difference is in our affective responses when the senses are triggered more directly. And our responsibility, painful as it might be, to seek out that directness as a form of ethical knowledge. I am reminded of a story Anne Carson tells in her remarkable book *NOX*, which is an elegy for her brother:

> When my brother died his dog got angry, stayed angry, barking, growling, lashing, glaring, by day and night. He went to the door, he went to the window, he would not lie down. My brother's widow, it is said, took the dog to the church on the day of the funeral. Buster goes right up to the front of Sankt Johannes and raises himself on his paws on the edge of the coffin and as soon as he smells the fact, his anger stops.

When I went down to the US-Mexico border in 2011 to understand better what was happening there, I saw many things that altered my sense of my belonging in the United States; not only my sense of belonging, but also my sense of responsibility. I saw people with swollen feet dropped back from a failed migration, cared for by volunteers in Mexico. In the United States, I saw border agents practicing their shooting at an open-air firing range. And I saw the border wall like a gash, like a wound, between the two. On a second visit to the border, I went to the county examiner's office in Tucson, and I was shown the bodies of the those who had died in the desert. Many would never be identified, their bodies too disfigured by wild birds, by wild dogs, by sun and wind and rain. That day, at the county examiner's office, I made a photograph of the unclaimed rows of the beloved dead. I remember that there was a faint smell of formaldehyde in the storage unit. But that was not the smell of death. I saw the fact, but I know I did not smell the fact. What would have happened had I smelled the fact?

More incisive (mysteriously so), more striking, more deeply into the fact, is something concerning the border that comes to me from a distance. I am thinking of something from late 2018, an event that stood as one in a string of those dispiriting moments that Adrienne Rich prophetically termed "our country moving closer to its own truth and dread." It was an audio recording surreptitiously made in a detention facility in Texas that June. In the recording we hear children between the ages of four and ten who are weeping, deeply distraught at having been separated from their parents. An agent, who can hear the raw pain of the kids, jokes, "We have an orchestra here." Seven minutes of very young children wailing and begging for their parents — *mami*, they cry out, *papa* — while all around them, the practical business of the border agents and consular officers continues. If one thinks, for a moment, of any child between the age of four and ten for whom one cares, the cruelty of the policy becomes unbearably apparent. The violence that subtends our societal arrangements can suddenly manifest through our hearing something, or seeing something, or perhaps most powerfully of all, smelling something.

This perhaps is the secret of someone like Caravaggio: that he can break through the surface of the canvas and evoke senses not normally connected to the art of painting. On the run for his life, he is as alive as he can bear to be, all across the spectrum of sense: sensate, sensitive, sensuous, sensual, sexual. Thinking about the bodies living and dead in Caravaggio sends me back to what Kristeva wrote: "Corpses show me what I permanently thrust aside in order to live." The smell of death, the smell of the fact, threatens one's identity. This is one of the key assertions in Kristeva's crucial essay *Powers of Horror*, from 1980, in which she lays out for us new thinking about the abject. "The corpse," she writes, "seen without God and outside of science, is the utmost abjection. It is death infecting life."

One account, probably apocryphal, says that Caravaggio had a recently buried corpse exhumed so he could use it as a model for his Lazarus. But in Caravaggio, the apocryphal and the real become very close. When we look at the rigor mortis of Lazarus, his greenish skin, we can almost smell the picture. Lazarus of Bethany, friend of Jesus, brother to Mary and Martha, is buried in a tomb sealed off with a stone. Jesus, seeing the distress of those who loved this man, is himself distressed; his power over life and death does not diminish his affective response. *Jesus wept.* The story is told in the eleventh chapter of the Gospel of John, and it is there that I find the detail that strikes me most powerfully: "Jesus, once more deeply moved, came to the tomb. It was a cave with a stone laid across the entrance. 'Take away the stone,' he said. 'But, Lord,' said Martha, the sister of the dead man, 'by this time there is a bad odor, for he has been there four days.'"

Duccio's *The Raising of Lazarus* is part of the predella of his

monumental altarpiece, the *Maestà* (plate 7). In Duccio's rendering of the event, we are at the moment of miracle. Mary, in red, on
her knees, pleads. Martha explains to Jesus that her brother has
been dead too long. The crowd throngs. And he who was dead
comes forth, wrapped like a mummy. In his eyes we see the confusion, and the softening of the confusion into something like life
(painting is its own miracle in the way that it can toggle between
two emotional states). And there's a further and unforgettable
detail in Duccio's panel. A young man, near the entrance of the
tomb, looks directly at Lazarus, but he has covered his nose and
mouth. It is a holy moment, but a stench is a stench. This young
man injects the scene with a sad and humane poignancy. In certain scenes of mourning, there are those who weep with abandon,
sometimes throwing themselves at the body. Often, these are the
most closely bereaved, who, in the loss, are at a loss of themselves.
But there are frequently others, who are also grieving but perhaps
with a bit more distance, a distance that allows them to take in
more than the loss, to take in the smell as well and to therefore
cover their noses. The figure overwhelmed by the stench of death.
Where have I seen this figure before?

There she is in Koen Wessing's photograph from the Nicara-
guan conflict, as published in Roland Barthes's *Camera Lucida*.
A dead child on the street covered in a sheet, a mother weeping
in the foreground, another woman, some steps behind, covering
her nose. And there they are in Susan Meiselas's photograph from
the same conflict. They cover their noses, sometimes their faces,
both in grief and in disgust. The bodies, of protesters against the
regime, have begin to putrefy. Perhaps it's significant that these
are *neighbors*, for you would not mind the smell—or there are
things you would find more urgent than the smell—if it were
your child. The gesture of covering one's nose or the moment of

being overwhelmed by the smell is a gesture that indicates a certain distance, and in this distance, as we note in the paintings of Lazarus by Duccio and Giotto, and in photographs of Nicaragua by Wessing and Meiselas, is a space for the spectator to enter. We cannot feel this particular mother's grief, this sister's loss, but we know what it means to be in community and at the same time be susceptible to olfactory stimuli. We can at least be neighbors.

People who are in a state of abjection are often the same people who are said to "threaten our security." And indeed, they do: they threaten our sense of ourself as secure, as non-abject. They show the loss of security that always threatens the human self. People we have made to suffer extremely are reminders of something of which we don't want to be reminded: that we can suffer extremely too. Our security is threatened not because there is something they will *do* to us, some kind of attack, but rather because of what we *are*: beings as vulnerable and insecure as they are. This is knowledge that must be suppressed at all costs, knowledge that is therefore met with disgust. The abject is disgusting because it comes from us, because it is our unstable selves externalized, the intimate fact we cannot bear to smell. This is what happened to me in Pozzallo, in Sicily, when I unexpectedly encountered a fenced-in parking lot on which migrant boats had been stored. I received and understood the sad reality of those boats with my intellect, but it was when I smelled them that I burst into tears.

The news asserts itself as a neutral report on the state of things, and elicits predictable responses. In fact, it is an elaborate enterprise driven by the predictability of the response. "A boat sank," a news report might say, "and 700 people died." The reader's response might be, "What a pity." "Thousands of people have died crossing the US-Mexico border." "So sad." What is inaudible in all this, and in almost all news, is any sense that the events are not simply unfortunate, that they are folded in with our actions, with the actions of our government, and bear on our personal responsibilities to each other.

. . .

In the fall of 2013, I visited the Palazzo Pitti in Florence, where I saw, among other paintings there, Caravaggio's *Sleeping Cupid*, painted in Malta. Emerging from the museum, walking into the warren of streets in front of it, I suddenly fell into intense and bittersweet feelings that I somehow knew were connected to a memory of my childhood in Lagos. I began to remember certain afternoons in the 1980s when, coming back from school, which was at the University of Lagos campus in Akoka, and heading home, which was across town in the then-tranquil neighborhood of Ikeja, we would occasionally stop at a stationery store in Yaba, where my brother and I would spend our hard-earned pocket money on rare pencils, boxes of pastels, sable brushes, and heavy cream-colored artists' papers.

My brother and I were both crazy about drawing and painting, from when I was around seven and when he was five, onward into our teens. We still are. He's an artist, and I dabble. Back then we loved nothing more than to test our mother's patience by dawdling in the stationery store. She would be waiting in the car, eager to get back to Ikeja after what would have been a very long working day. But for my brother and I, the ritual of buying art materials was not to be rushed. We'd examine pencils in the hard H series (2H, 4H, 6H) and the soft B series (2B, 4B, 6B, and so on). Like all fanatics, we gloried in the specifics and went lovingly from aisle to aisle, consuming with our eyes and touching with our fingers the arrayed products, made by companies whose names were mantras to us, two little boys on a school afternoon in Lagos, manufacturers like Staedtler, Winsor & Newton, Rotring, Stabilo, and Faber-Castell, names that held for us the holy hush of promise, of hours of pleasure to come when we set up our easels and sketchbooks at home and, like the rivals we were, drew and painted still-life arrangements. But in that shop in Yaba, the name of which is now sadly lost to me, we would eventually have to make a decision and settle on what to buy.

The reality was that we never had much money. We might be able to afford the sixteen-pastel set, but not the glorious one with sixty-four sticks. We might have enough money for the horsehair brush, but not the real sable brush, the one that, when wetted, took on the shape of a teardrop that terminated in a single point. So, on each visit, desire would meet limitations, and we would have to spend within our means. We took our time deciding. Afterward, we headed out to the car and our mother, whose patience had likely expired. Of course we knew that the happiness that would come from one new brush or a new set of pencils was more than worth our mother's temporary displeasure. Besides, she took a secret pride in our artistic abilities, since she had no such facility herself, and sometimes mused on the mystery of having children with inclinations so radically different from hers.

All of this came rushing back that afternoon in Florence. And it wasn't the memories themselves that suddenly overwhelmed me, it was the *feelings* associated with those memories, those intense and bittersweet feelings. I felt unaccountably young, happy, full of anticipation, overstimulated, competitive, creative, and vulnerable, and only after a few moments did the reason for those feelings reveal itself in the memory of visiting the stationery shop. Where had this torrent of feeling suddenly come from, almost thirty years later and thousands of miles away, in a foreign country? What could have triggered such powerful associations? I turned around in the small Florentine street, walked back a few steps, and found the answer: I had smelled the fragrance of freshly shaved pencils. Amazing, that in the cacophony of the street, I could be felled by something so faint and specific. I had walked by a shop selling art materials, and the smell coming from its open doors had served as a shuttle to my boyhood self. The sensation of smell had bypassed my conscious mind, gone deep to the root of my memory, and given me an experience stronger than that I'd got from the masterful paintings with which I had just spent the afternoon, the works of Giovanni Bellini, Raphael, Titian, Caravaggio.

Henry de Montherlant is credited with saying that "happiness writes in white ink on a white page," but I believe that happiness is no less complex an emotion than sorrow. The abject smell that broke my heart in Pozzallo, the painting of St John's beheading in Malta, the videos and voices from Libya, and the crying of bereft children on the recording from Texas: these are all news from the unhappy side of life. Each is powerful and unforgettable in its own way. But the sweet smell of shaved pencils on a Florentine street is as profound as any of them. Our senses are unendingly intricate and subtle. We can see, we can hear, we can touch and be touched, we can taste, we can smell. We know where the parts of our body are, we can feel hot and cold, we can feel pain, we can maintain our balance. We can experience moments of synesthesia, we can be astonished by the smell of jasmine, we can be moved by the sound of drums, we can feel the way architecture acts on the body. We can find, in book after book, in film after film, those moments of complexity and complication that shake us awake and bind us ever more closely to life, those embodied and neurological experiences that reassure us that we are not alone.

Moving through the world, finely tuned, encountering others who are also finely tuned, their bodies mingled with ours, their intricacy and subtlety: all of this bears on our ethical responsibility toward those others. It is as though we are all in the same boat and, in that same boat, we can smell each others' bodies. In *Regarding the Pain of Others*, Susan Sontag sounds a helpful note of caution: "Compassion is an unstable emotion. It needs to be translated into action, or it withers. The question is what to do with the feelings that have been aroused, the knowledge that has been communicated. People don't become inured to what they are shown—if that's the right way to describe what happens—because of the quantity of images dumped on them. It is passivity that dulls feeling." I'm interested in what Sontag terms "passivity" here. The quantity of images, she suggests, is not what is at issue. What is at issue is the way they are received. How can the recipient of this fact of the world be more active?

I often think that if sensitivity is a feature of my ethical equipment, then the same must be true for others. I don't mean that exquisite sensitivity is required in order to be morally alert. I mean that it can function as a reminder, as an intensifier, of what we have always owed each other. To paraphrase Édouard Glissant, when we regard each other, we should tremble. These are the reasons I travel, or read, or look at art: to find out, to feel, to tremble, to forestall any risk that the active fact might be rendered passive or useless. I open myself up to shake off "raising awareness" and take on "bearing witness," to go closer, to feel what I feel there (wherever "there" may be), to observe what I sense and transmute that into shared responsibility, into a knowledge that my body—our bodies—were made fit for it.

PART FIVE

IN A DARK TIME

A Time for Refusal

It is a Sunday afternoon in a provincial town in France. Two men
meet at a cafe. One of them, Berenger, is half-drunk. He is being
berated by his companion, Jean. All of the sudden, they hear a
great noise. When they and other townspeople crane their necks
to figure out what's going on, they see a large animal thundering
down one of the streets, stamping and snorting all the way. A rhinoceros! Not long after, there's another. They are startled. It's outrageous. Something must be done. What they begin to do is argue
heatedly about whether the second rhino was the first one going
past a second time or a different one, and then about whether the
rhinos are African or Asiatic.

Things become more disturbing in the next act. (This is a play:
Rhinoceros, written by Eugène Ionesco.) The rhino sightings continue to be the subject of pointless dispute. Then, one by one,
various people in the town begin to turn into rhinos. Their skin
hardens, bumps appear over their noses and grow into horns. Jean
had been one of those scandalized by the first two rhino sightings,
but he becomes a rhino, too. Midway through his metamorphosis, Berenger argues with him: "You must admit that we have a

philosophy that animals don't share, and an irreplaceable set of values, which it's taken centuries of human civilization to build up." Jean, well on his way to being a rhino, retorts, "When we've demolished all that, we'll be better off!"

It is an epidemic of "rhinoceritis." Almost everyone succumbs: those who admire the brute force of the rhinos, those who didn't believe the sightings to begin with, those who initially found them alarming. One character, Dudard, declares, "If you're going to criticize, it's better to do so from the inside." And so he willingly undergoes the metamorphosis, and there's no way back for him. The final holdouts from this mass capitulation are Berenger and Daisy, his coworker.

Eugène Ionesco, who was French-Romanian, wrote *Rhinoceros* in 1958 as a response to totalitarian movements in Europe, but he was influenced specifically by his experience of fascism in Romania in the 1930s. Ionesco wanted to know why so many people give in to these poisonous ideologies. How could so many get it so wrong? The play, a farce, was one way he grappled with this problem.

On August 19, 2015, shortly after midnight, brothers Stephen and Scott Leader assaulted a man named Guillermo Rodriguez, who had been sleeping near a train station in Boston. The Leader brothers beat him with a metal pipe, breaking his nose and bruising his ribs, and called him a "wetback." They urinated on him. "All these illegals need to be deported," they are said to have declared during the attack. The brothers were fans of the candidate who would go on to win the Republican Party's presidential nomination. Told of the incident at the time, that candidate said: "People who are following me are very passionate. They love this country, and they want this country to be great again."

That was the moment when my mental alarm bells, already

ringing, went amok. There were many other astonishing events to come—the accounts of sexual violence, the evidence of racism, the promise of torture, the advocacy of war crimes—but the assault on Rodriguez, and the largely tolerant response to it, was a marker. Some people were outraged, but outrage soon became its own ineffectual reflex. Others found a rich vein of humor in the parade of obscenities and cruelties. Others took a view similar to that of the character Botard in Ionesco's play: "I don't mean to be offensive. But I don't believe a word of it. No rhinoceros has ever been seen in this country!"

In the early hours of November 9, 2016, the winner of the presidential election was declared. As the day unfolded, the extent to which a moral rhinoceritis had taken hold was apparent. *People* magazine had a giddy piece about the president-elect's daughter and her family, a sequence of photos it headlined "way too cute." In the *New York Times*, one opinion piece suggested that the belligerent bigot's supporters ought not to be shamed. Another asked whether this president-elect could be a good president and found cause for optimism. Cable news anchors found means to express their surprise at the outcome of the election, but no way to vocalize their fury. All around were the unmistakable signs of normalization in progress. So many were falling into line without being pushed. It was happening at tremendous speed, like a contagion. And it was catching even those whose plan was, like Dudard's in *Rhinoceros*, to criticize "from the inside."

Evil settles into everyday life when people are unable or unwilling to recognize it. It makes its home among us when we are keen to minimize it or describe it as something else. This is not a process that began a week or a month or a year ago. It did not begin with drone assassinations, or with the war on Iraq. Evil has always been here. But now it has taken on a totalitarian tone.

At the end of *Rhinoceros*, Daisy finds the call of the herd ir-
resistible. Her skin goes green, she develops a horn, she's gone.
Berenger, imperfect, all alone, is racked by doubts. He is determined to keep his humanity, but looking in the mirror, he suddenly finds himself quite strange. He feels like a monster for being
so out of step with the consensus. He is afraid of what this inde-
pendence will cost him. But he keeps his resolve and refuses to
accept the horrible new normalcy. He'll put up a fight, he says.
"I'm not capitulating!"

Resist, Refuse

The courage of the French Resistance, a courage immeasurably beyond chatter and imposture, helped make "resistance" a holy word in our common tongue. We look back on these people — many of whom were caught, most of whom were tortured and executed soon after they were caught — with frightened admiration. Facing the unspeakable, they committed themselves to the unimaginable.

But "resistance" is back in vogue, and it describes something rather different. The holy word has become unexceptional. Faced with a vulgar, manic, and cruel regime, birds of many different feathers are eager to proclaim themselves members of "the Resistance." It is the most popular game in town. Membership in an actual Resistance cell was no game. The *réseau* Gloria SMH for instance: betrayed to the Gestapo by the double agent Father Robert Alesch in 1942. Twelve members were shot, more than eighty others tortured and sent to Buchenwald and Mauthausen. Only an early warning saved Suzanne Déchevaux-Dumesnil and her companion Samuel Beckett. They escaped to a free zone. Many others in the network died; these two lived, somehow.

You can sense this nearness to death (the absurdity of having escaped death) in Beckett's postwar work, beginning with his stories of 1946. The work is full of questions about what can be said and what cannot. He turns definitively to writing in French after the war to free himself of English, to strip down his language. It is a fulfillment of something he had written in a 1937 letter: "More and more my own language appears to me like a veil that must be torn apart in order to get at the things (or the Nothingness) behind it." The writing becomes more obsessive, more doubtful, more pained, less decorative. It is arid for long stretches, seldom dealing with actual matters of the war. This is the writing of a man who has seen too much.

When I think about the atmosphere of the French Resistance, I also think of Jean-Pierre Melville's *Army of Shadows* (1969), a somber and intense film that presents heroism in an unusual way: not as a thrill but as a simultaneously heavy and utterly ordinary set of choices. A pilot, a housewife, a philosopher: we are drawn into their world in order to see how they are like us and how, mysteriously, they have chosen risk instead of safety. Their heroism, like that of many in the Resistance, finally comes to nothing. There's betrayal. Most of them die.

This was resistance without merriment, abjuring any gestures of entertainment. The Resistance did not even come with the assurance that it would be strategically effective (the French Resistance was not a unified force with a single coherent set of tactics). So, why did they do it? The writer and resister Roger Stéphane put it this way in 1952: "Never had so many men consciously run so many risks for such a small thing: a desire to bear witness. Perhaps it is absurd, but it was by such absurdities that we restored our dignity as men."

A dangerous commitment to resistance made by hundreds of

thousands, tens of thousands of whom died in France alone. For a spell in the early 1940s, whenever the members of the Resistance killed a Nazi, the Nazis would execute fifty innocent French; an unspeakable calculus, but it did not stop the Resistance (its Communist wing in particular) from killing Nazis. It was a terrible time. The Resistance recognized that what was as stake was not just political power but also human dignity, which, all question of tactical efficacy aside, the resisters saw as non-negotiable.

This history looms each time the word "resistance" is evoked in American politics. This history judges the triviality of our responses, judges us for making a sacred word banal and dulling its intensity. The triviality of our response is not in the predicament of so many who have died here already, nor is it in the serious work being undertaken by so many people far from the spotlight. It is to be found in the voices of those who set the public tone. How I long now, on behalf of America, for Beckett's aridity, for Melville's gloom, for Stéphane's desire to bear witness, for a sobriety of affect that matches the enormity of the crime. How are we to live in this? How are we to inhabit the principle behind the word "resistance" when the meaning of the word itself has changed so much? What are we to do in a nation that surpasses all others in turning suffering into entertainment?

I propose a resistance made of refusals. Refuse a resistance excised of courage. Refuse the conventional arena and take the fight elsewhere. Refuse to eat with the enemy, refuse to feed the enemy. Refuse to participate in the logic of the crisis, refuse to be reactive to its provocations. Refuse to forget last year's offenses and last month's and last week's. Refuse the news cycle, refuse commentary. Refuse to place newsworthiness above human solidarity. Refuse to be intimidated by pragmatism. Refuse to be judged by cynics. Refuse to be too easily consoled. Refuse to admire mere political survival. Refuse to accept the calculation of the lesser evil. Refuse nostalgia. Refuse to laugh along. Refuse the binary of the terrible past and the atrocious present. Refuse to ignore the plight of the imprisoned, the tortured and the deported. Refuse to be mesmerized by shows of power. Refuse the mob. Refuse to play, refuse decorum, refuse accusation, refuse distraction, which is a tolerance of death-dealing by another name. And when told you can't refuse, refuse that, too.

Through the Door

Growing up in Lagos, Nigeria, I lived with my parents and siblings in a two-bedroom rental in a middle-class section of the city, on the top floor of a three-story house. This was around 1981. My mother was a French teacher. Perhaps, if she'd not had the care of myself and my siblings, if things had gone differently, she'd have been a diplomat. My father was a midlevel manager in a multinational cocoa-processing company. His job took him out of the country often. He went to Ghana, Cote d'Ivoire, Korea, the UK, and, most frequently, Brazil. We did not own our home, did not even own land, but once, returning from Brazil, my father brought a door back with him: a beautiful wooden door of stained teak, a deep honey color, luminous, gorgeous.

It was a mystery, and it was slightly absurd, this buying of a door. My father had spent all this money on a magnificent door that he'd had shipped from São Paulo. He'd also bought heavy brass handles, and locks, and a baroque brass door knocker in the shape of a lion's head that had already acquired a dark patina. Door and door handle and door knocker fit for a cathedral, along with locks and keys and hinges, all bought by a man who owned no land. We kept the door in a side room and it gathered dust. A friend and colleague of his, who was building a house, saw the door. This friend said, "That's a beautiful door. Tell you what, let me buy it from you." My father said no. "I'll pay a lot for it," his friend said. "It really is very beautiful." Not at any price, my father said.

My father's quixotic commitment, fully supported by my mother, to an actual door for an unbuilt house on an as-yet-imaginary plot of land has stayed with me, not only as an act of faith, but as proof of an instinct for understanding the symbolic power of portals. I love the ambiguity inherent in "door" and "doorway." If someone says, "It's the door on your left," they mean, "It's the doorway on your left." A door is always taking you out and bringing you in, even when it's taking you out of the inside and bringing you in to the outside. It is in this sense a reflexive technology. A door is a threshold, a through-point, a site of potential, imbued with transitional energies. It is the zone of crossings, of what is soon to be but not yet, the kingdom of the ambiguous god Hermes. A door is—to get down to the dictionary definition—a movable barrier, usually on hinges, demarcating one side of a wall from another. (Ogden Nash had a funny definition of door: "A door is whatever a dog is on the wrong side of.") The idea of a door as an opportunity, the symbolic idea, is also very old, maybe only five minutes younger than the door as a physical object. It's an obvious metaphor the way a road is an obvious metaphor, and our ancestors immediately saw it.

. . .

In 1401, there was a competition for the redesign of the doors of the ancient octagonal baptistery that stood opposite the cathedral in Florence. The applicants submitted their entries, high-relief quatrefoil bronze castings on a set subject: the sacrifice of Isaac. There were seven semifinalists, five of whom fell by the wayside, and Lorenzo Ghiberti and Filippo Brunelleschi were named the finalists. They were both in their early twenties at the time.

Brunelleschi's conception of the sacrifice of Isaac was bold, highly dramatic, Abraham's arm outstretched, the angel flying in from the left side of the panel. Ghiberti's was more rhythmic and elegant, fine in detail, more unified compositionally, responsive to the graceful curves of the International Gothic style. The jury couldn't decide. They named the men joint winners, and proposed that they work together to design the reliefs for the massive doors. Ghiberti was fine with it, but Brunelleschi was incensed. He thought *he* should have been the clear winner and he withdrew in a sulk. Ghiberti designed the doors, in gilded bronze, a labor of twenty-one years, and they can still be seen on the north façade of the Baptistery. So extraordinary are they that he was commissioned to do the east doors as well. That took him another twenty-seven years, and they were even better. As for Brunelleschi, he was so upset that he quit sculpture and headed to Rome to study architecture. It was he who discovered one-point linear perspective. It was he who designed the dome of the Duomo, still the largest brick vault in the world. He is considered the father of Renaissance architecture.

Not a whole lot comes up when you dig into the etymology of the word "door." Proto-Germanic *Dur*, Old Frisian *Dore*, Proto-Indo-European *dhwer*. The general sense is that "door" in Proto-Indo-European meant a pair of doors, possibly swinging doors. So, "door" means "two doors," which doesn't give us much. But it tells us how old the word is, and how old its sense is in human civilization. Like *hand*, like *bread*, like *home*: these are words we've had as long as we've had words, because we've needed them as long as we've done language.

Theophilus van Kannel, a Philadelphian, was reputed to hate chivalry. Holding the doors for ladies and such courtliness: he just wasn't into it. "After you, please." "No, after *you*, please." In 1888, van Kannel improved on an invention by H. Bockhacker, filing a patent for a "storm door-structure." It was an energy saver, and of great help in particularly busy places. Van Kannel's door is what we know today as a revolving door. This is door as continuous loop, always opening and always closing, and always, perhaps, on the verge of making one dizzy or leading to a comic disaster.

Doors also bring to mind simpler, less high-tech moments. One could think of a house as a set of walls surmounted by a roof. The house could almost do without windows. What it *must* have, though, is a door. A house without a doorway, a house without a door, is either a dungeon or a tomb. To be a proper machine for living, it must afford traffic. I love the simplicity and intensity with which Peter Zumthor describes his pre-architectural sensitivity to the material world. He writes:

> There was a time when I experienced architecture without thinking about it. Sometimes I can almost feel a particular door handle in my hand, a piece of metal shaped like the back of a spoon. I used to take hold of it when I went into my aunt's garden. That door handle still seems to me like a special sign of entry into a world of different moods and smells.

Underneath the technical learning that goes into architecture is the desire to create work that is experienced materially and without affectation, work that is resonant on a precognitive level, like the door handle Zumthor's aunt affixed to her garden gate, or the door that traveled from one rental to another with my family for close to a decade of my childhood. German "door" is *Tür*. But *durch* is German for through, and this leads me back to the English "through"—from one side to the other, crossing over, to overcome—which indeed is from the same etymological root as "door": door and doorway are one.

. . .

A few years ago, I traveled overland from Lagos across the so-called Slave Coast in West Africa, through Cotonou until my companions and I arrived at Ouidah, in the Benin Republic. This was a journey into traces of human cruelty. We saw the tree where enslaved people had been chained; we saw the holding pen, now a mere field, where thousands had been held; we saw the pit into which the rebellious among them had been thrown to their deaths. Finally, looking out to sea, was a modern structure, an arch of concrete and bronze, called the Door of No Return. A door of no return is a contradiction in terms, dousing the generosity of portals, making of them a one-way horror, and it was this horror that the arch commemorated.

The door of contradiction in Ouidah leads my thoughts to a work by the American artist Robert Gober, *Untitled Door and Door Frame*. This is a startling installation in which an open doorway directs our attention to a door on the facing wall. It is like a thought that leads nowhere but back to itself, a kind of pun on how a door is a synonym for a doorway. Gober's door is a version of the anti-door of the forts of Gorée and Ouidah; doorness deconstructed, a powerful, puzzling work.

· · ·

Many years later, my parents finally bought a piece of land. It was a modest parcel, way on the outskirts of Lagos. The area, back then, was practically still forested. But by degrees, the land was cleared. Foundations were made, walls raised, lintels established, a roof, a porch, and finally, like a jewel in a velvet cushion, the magnificent door from Brazil was set into the frame of the doorway. Its leonine brass knocker was affixed. Because the door was real in 1981, the house became real in 1989. When I left home in 1992 and set out on my American journey at the age of seventeen, it was through that doorway, literally. I stepped out the beautiful, long-nurtured Brazilian door, headed to the Lagos airport, flew to America, began a new phase of life. One door and then another, and then another, through my studies and through my books, the many doors of life, one door and then another, and then another, through my doubts and moments of despair, through my searches, and through my many cities, through the doors that brought me to the present moment. Such is the power of symbolic thinking.

This, finally, brings to mind an incident from this current dispensation, in which our country moves closer to its point of no return. On the US-Mexico border, in the San Diego Sector, the wall winds across the terrain like a scar. At Border Field State Park, the wall is like a security fence. In the wall is embedded a door, a gate. Since 2013, under the aegis of a nonprofit called Border Angels, that door has briefly swung open six times. They call it the Door of Hope. People from Tijuana and people from San Diego meet each other there, for a hug, for a kiss, for a limited family reunion.

Without those on either side crossing over, long-separated people are reunited for some precious moments. In November 2017, there was even a wedding there, between Brian Houston, of

Rancho San Diego, and Evelia Reyes, of Tijuana, under the unsmiling eyes of the Border Patrol. And then in January 2018, because our own country is moving closer to its own ways of making people disappear, the Door of Hope was permanently shut, as though kindness itself had been an offense, as though grace itself had been an intolerable oversight. That open door had represented a state of exception, a grace note in a brutal regime of division. This was not where people migrated. It was on no smuggler's path. It was merely a place of some few, brief, happy tears, a crack in the wall through which the light could get in.

Passages North

1

She works up north, near Svalbard, putting small rocks to her tongue. By taste she can identify which are calcified, which, in other words, are not mere rocks but possibly fossils. She is a paleontologist. The country is old. There was life here.

Life of a different kind hides in the Svalbard Global Seed Vault, an ark for the future of humanity. There is, will be, life here. It is a vault that imagines a cataclysm yet to come, a vault Norway hosts on behalf of humanity. A thought experiment made real, in the keeping of the earth. A lever point.

The paleontologist is married to Andreas.

2

The summer has been dry. The fields look scorched (as blond as the groups of women I will later see walking down Bogstadveien). Andreas tells me that if there had been any doubt before, if the rules of evidence were sufficiently complex that one couldn't say of any given weather spike that it was caused by climate change, all such doubt is now gone. This is the first year, he says, that one can say for sure and fear no contradiction that the climate has changed, that, without a doubt, things are getting hotter. As he speaks, I watch a man walk across a field, a man lit by the late afternoon's glare.

3

On the way back, on the ferry back, we are three. I ask Andreas if he thinks that the man taking us across — who had also brought us inbound — is the same man who brought the killer across that day. Andreas is quiet for a moment. There is great stillness on this water across which dozens swam. Many made it to safety; many didn't. Andreas says, It could be him. He has worked here for decades. It's likely to be him, he says, but I wouldn't want to ask.

4

"Ut" for *out*, "øya" for *island*: the outer island, the outermost and smallest of three. Storøya, big isle. Geitøya, goat isle. Later, I am surprised to find that many of the people I talk to in Oslo have not been to Utøya. Forty minutes from the city, but it is like a mythical island: thought and dreamed and argued about and wept over. Just before going to Utøya, I attempt to talk myself out of it. Why would you go there, why would you do such a thing? To see what? To do what? But I know this voice by now, a counterpoint to the other, stronger voice that often urges me to go where things have happened. I might buy books about the things that happened, but I always leave them unread until I physically feel the terrain.

Andreas has driven me from Oslo to Utstranda, from which we take the ferry. We arrive on a fine day in late August and are met by Jørgen, who directs activities on the island. (He came into the job in 2011, shortly after the day of the attack.) Walking around the island, this small island as still in the August air as a held breath. Walking on the Lovers' Path along the water and

above the low cliffs where eleven young people laid down in stillness by the water pump. Stillness, hoping the killer would not
notice them, by the water pump, where he walked up on their
prone bodies and began shooting.

Out here on the out island.

5

On the Tyrifjorden, I recall that nowhere in *The Odyssey* or *The
Iliad* does Homer say "blue." A perfect blue day, a blue so overwhelming that it is like the blue before language for blue arrives.

The cafeteria stood and now stands under the blue sky. It is
surrounded by the Hegnhuset, shield house, whose columns of
thicker wood are sixty-nine in number, the slenderer columns
surrounding them four hundred and ninety-five. The dead, sixty-
nine of them, hold up the roof. The living, four hundred and
ninety-five, surround the dead. Only humans do this. We shield
our dead. They keep us sheltered.

6

While we are on the island, Andreas says, Art is the remembrance
of the details, those details you can't possibly remember. I ask him
to say it again, and I write it down: Art is the remembrance of the
details, those details you can't possibly remember.

7

I have met four Andreases. It's as though everyone is named
Andreas. One I meet just in passing, the other three I get to know
and have real conversations with. The different Andreases tell me
different stories. Distinct but continuous Andreases.

When I was growing up, Andreas says, very few people were
named Andreas. Now, when I'm walking past a kindergarten, I

might hear a voice saying, Andreas, stop it, get down from that table, and for a moment I think, That's me!

8

I don't know Ludvig Holberg, other than that he was an early notable intellectual in Norway, a philosopher and playwright. But I love the music by Grieg devoted to him: *From Holberg's Time*, subtitled "Suite in olden style." I like it even more than I like the better known incidental music to *Peer Gynt*. There's a beautiful and yearning quality to the Holberg Suite, a dreamspace I occupied and reoccupied both before and during my time in Oslo.

My room is only two stops by tram from Holbergs Plass. Andreas mentions in passing that Ludvig Holberg, a canny investor, certainly put quite a bit of money into slaving ships and reaped the rewards. Later I discover that Holberg had his own "Black man" — a man enslaved in his house.

And one must now recall that nearly a hundred thousand people were transported across the Atlantic on Danish and Norwegian ships between 1670 and 1802. From Copenhagen, liquor and weapons to Africa; from the Gold Coast, enslaved people to the Caribbean; from the Caribbean, sugar, tobacco, and mahogany back to Europe. The so-called triangular trade.

The Holberg Suite is in five movements, full of character and feeling.

9

I recall in Denmark a Dane saying to me, We don't care for the Swedes, but we really like the Norwegians. My response: And the Norwegians, what do they think of you? And her response: Oh. I hadn't thought of that. I don't know. I hope they like us.

10

A party at Østgaards Gate. Because I am a guest and a foreigner, I break protocol and ask some of the other visitors what political parties they belong to. This is not a question they would ask each other, and this is not a question I would ask at an American party. But because I am a guest and a foreigner, because there are in-conveniences that I want to make visible, I break protocol. They tell me: Social left. Labour. Social left. Red. Green Party. Liberal. And in the briefest and most fleeting moment, you can see their mutual disappointments. My questioning almost spoils the party.

I'm struck by something written in the *New York Times* when the conservatives won in 2017. Harald Baldersheim, a professor emeritus of political science at the University of Oslo, was quoted as saying, "From a comparative perspective, Norwegian poli-tics has never been — and is not — very polarized. Both blocs are gravitating toward the center. In this sense, not much is at stake."

I'm not a professor of political science, but I've been haunted by the phrase *not much is at stake*. Is that true? Could that be true? There's not very much at stake for whom? What is at stake for the Black Norwegian who grows up with the nationalist Progress Party sharing power? Professor Baldersheim added, "The four years of coalition government has tamed the Progress Party and made it harmless." Is that the truth? How is harmlessness defined here? What is at stake when the rhetoric of the government di-minishes your being and your presence? It is precisely at the mar-gins that a society's wounds split open.

11

The hours after the attack. Something terrible has happened, something unspeakable. Many are dead. There are families who will never be whole again. (Too frequently we have to confront these thoughts.) I wasn't in Norway when the killer struck. But I was in New York on the day of mayhem there, in Nairobi during the massacre there. Something terrible happens, and I am left with the feeling of having been close to it and of having escaped only by chance.

On July 22, who and what and why—even on a basic level—are all still hours from being known. In these first few hours in the city, there are random acts of violence against the "other." Against Muslims, against Somalis, those who are deemed likely to have committed the atrocity. (This is before it emerges that the killer was motivated precisely by hatred of the Muslim other.)

In these first few hours on the island, where the majority of the dead lie, the frantic calling by parents and loved ones makes the abandoned cellphones ring in the dark, the displays of light coming and going like clouds of fireflies, then the ringing getting fainter and fewer as the phone batteries drain away.

12

The Regjeringskvartalet, the Government Quarter, emanates a post-traumatic feeling. Under construction, under wraps, as though manifesting, in physical form, that which cannot be spoken about.

13

Fiction is made up and so cannot really be erroneous. We understand it as taking place in a universe quite similar to ours, extensively similar in fact, but with a few deviations: of character, or place. I write about a nonexistent place, a town in Norway that a secondary character hails from. But this nonexistent or, rather, misnamed place bothers me in a way that the invented streets do not, for the latter are invented intentionally and the former is a mistake.

Here's what happened: I did not want my character Lise to be from Oslo, Lillehammer, Trondheim, or anywhere too obvious, so I had her place of origin be a name I'd heard only in music: Troldhaugen. But I was to later discover that Troldhaugen isn't a town or even a village. It's the composer's home, it's Grieg's name for his home in Bergen. "Troldhaugen"—the name of a home, not of a town—remains in the book like an unpaid debt.

14

Andreas says that in the eighteenth century, one of his ancestors, a barber-surgeon, out in the hinterland of the country, rendered a medical service to a visiting Dutch sailor. This sailor rewarded his ancestor with a young Black boy. The boy became a member of Andreas's ancestor's family, less an enslaved person and more an adopted son, and it was thought that rather than be merely a barber-surgeon he ought to go to the city of Christiania (as Oslo was known back then) to attend the medical school there and become a proper doctor. The boy went. He enrolled in the medical faculty. Then the historical trace disappears.

The young man returns to the village, and he has not become a doctor. Was he expelled for his race? Did he leave of his own accord? He becomes a barber-surgeon like his adopted father.

It is said that he left no descendants in the family, though it is also said that, on visits to the outlying farmsteads and villages, he had encounters with certain maidens and that children were born to them. Evidence has emerged, Andreas told me, that he was not, in fact, of African descent. He was Filipino, a victim of the Dutch trade in the East Indies.

15

Joachim Trier's *Oslo, August 31st* was released on August 31, 2011. It is screened in Oslo on August 31 each year. Summer is ending. The swimming pools close. The weather shifts. A sad and very beautiful film.

After a conversation with Anne Hilde on August 31, 2018, I realize that the café featured in the film is actually — quite by chance — opposite the Litteraturhuset, and that I've been looking at it every day from my window. In a sense, I had watched the film and the film had watched me. And so I go into the café for a moment, close my eyes, and listen.

16

The lead in *Oslo, August 31st* is Anders Danielsen Lie. The film is an account of a day in the life of the character. On August 31, 2018, I'm walking around the city, and it's as though I am following Anders. (The character is given the actor's own name.) No, not following him. I do not actually retrace his paths or go to the places he goes. But I feel in myself the undeniable power of a series of encounters and sights compressed into a single day.

Early on in the film, there's a powerful scene set in a café in which the depressed Anders picks up, through overheard fragments, the ways in which other people carry on with their lives. He listens.

Earlier, Anders had said to his friend Thomas, "If you're unsentimental about it, nobody needs me. Not really." We know the statement is untrue, but we also know that in the grip of depression — a depression in Anders's case exacerbated by drug addiction and a failed effort at rehab — other truths impose themselves.

It is interesting to think of Joachim Trier's powerful film on the one hand and, on the other, the 2017 declaration that Norway was the happiest country in the world. There are ways in which both the melancholy and felicity are true of Norway. In any case, there are happy countries and there are countries with happy people, and perhaps the two do not perfectly overlap. Perhaps Norway is a happy country with unhappy people.

I find myself more convinced by the idea that we navigate our lives individually, whatever the country, and that those complexities and pains cannot be accounted for by polls. Sorrow is not an economic metric.

17

All cities are continuations of other cities. Virtually all are subject to the same neoliberal arrangements, so that whether or not the water supply is good or the electrical grid is reliable, you'll still find Burger King and the Body Shop and H&M and IKEA. In any given city, as I wander around, there are moments of self-forgetfulness. Where am I? Is this São Paulo or Lagos? Is this Copenhagen or Oslo? Is this Chicago, Stavanger, Milan, Auckland? The languages are dialects, the neighborhoods are profiles from a common kaleidoscope.

Nevertheless, as I watch the sun rise and set on Parkveien and Bogstadveien, I know that in this corner of this city, there are specific histories overlaid on specific histories — someone's daily path to work, a shop someone cannot bear to enter because it is too full of memories, someone's first kiss, the corner where an accident happened, a club where a couple met for the first time and began a life together, the traffic light someone was standing at when they heard about July 22; and then, in an even deeper vein of history, the fading experiences of parents, grandparents, the emigrants, the lives they lived, the War Years, the unforgettable winters, the city of Christiania and the hilly terrain well before it was called Oslo, and well before it was a city, and far beyond that, the Viking Law.

18

Walking with Christian through the National Gallery, he asks me about my relationship to painting. He knows I have been photographing details of paintings all year. I tell him that one impetus for the project was the work of Edvard Munch, which I had seen in New York the previous December, the way his details are so painterly. Munch's work tends to be representational, but any given detail has the possibility of holding its own as an abstract painting. A second impetus, I tell Christian, is that in certain films I love, films by Andrei Tarkovsky or Michael Haneke, for instance, the camera from time to time comes to rest on a painting. These moments are non-narrative and do not advance the plot. They are instances of pastoral, which might be accompanied by music (Tarkovsky) or silence (Haneke).

A filmic view of a landscape is not quite the same as a filmic view of a painting. The landscape is always charged with the possibility of usefulness. When you're looking at a field, someone can always walk across that field. A painting, on the other hand, is settled. It is there to be looked at. It stills the frenzy of the human heart. It declares a zone of compassion. Without clamor, enclosed in a frame.

19

I walk around not really knowing what I am looking at. I have been to Oslo before, once. The streets, the shops, the stations, the many bits of familiar city logic. But in this case, because I want to write some things down, I am asking myself what it is possible to understand in such a short time. Part of understanding is to embrace the "not understanding," to inhabit a feeling of uncompletable understanding. A photograph I made at the Oslo Opera House was a photo of not understanding. But soon after, the tenor of the next photographs changed: they became photographs not of not understanding but of a limited understanding. I stare for hours at the photographs I have made in Norway. They seem to know more than I do. Slow-release images.

20

One of the challenges of photography is that it seeks to make the world a spectacle. I want to push past the spectacular. This process is so difficult that I sometimes feel I might as well be photographing with my eyes closed.

In many essays that talk about "the essay," authors point out that the root of the word *essay* is the French infinitive *essayer*: to try or to attempt. (This is such a cliché by now that I look out for it in essays about essaying, the way one searches, preemptively and irritably, for a shot of the Eiffel Tower in films set in Paris.)

How can a photo be an attempt? How do we retain in a photo the tension and openness of an essay? A photo that does essaywork must remain unresolved, unfinished; it must continue to attempt.

21

We look at the world while thinking our thoughts, thoughts that may by chance match the world we are looking at, or that may be independent of it. What is seen and what is said are in the same universe. The universe is enclosed, the permutations infinite.

22

While we are on Utøya, looking across the water, he tells me about his daughter. She was born blind and deaf, and it is a mystery how she can reach the world and how the world can reach her. But she knows of their love, and they know of hers.

We who live in these bodies. How little we suspect of the burden of care.

23

In Oslo, she tells me about her father, dying now, possibly dying, in a suburban hospital. She enters the hospital room and there is a woman there (a beautiful woman, she says) whom she doesn't know. The woman is speaking to her father in an intimate way, it seems, her father who is comatose. I'm his daughter, she tells the woman. I worked with him for a decade, the woman says.

The beautiful woman continues to speak to her father, and she is watching the woman speak to her father, and she thinks that she sees her father's hand move (he is comatose but has moments of wakefulness). Her father's hand, she thinks, lifts slowly, touches the beautiful woman's bottom—the woman does not react and is not surprised—and slowly returns to its place, her father who is dying.

24

At the National Museum, in front of the most famous painting in Scandinavia, I see one tourist after another pose for a picture. They pose in front of *The Scream* in the silent pretense of a scream, hands held up to faces.

Perhaps I am thinking about the ongoing disaster in American politics. Perhaps I am thinking about the slow-motion disaster everywhere, and the real pains that come with it, the wounded, the wounding continual. In any case, I cannot enter into the spirit of pretend screaming but am instead reminded again of the words Aimé Césaire wrote in his *Notebook of a Return to the Native Land*:

> Beware of assuming the sterile attitude of a spectator, for life is not a spectacle . . . a man screaming is not a dancing bear . . .

25

At the jazz bar Herr Nilsen on a Sunday, the stage is open for a variety of bands. It is a cool and unpretentious place with good beer and decent wine. Several trios and quartets play, and there's one particularly fine pianist.

In the small audience, comprising maybe twenty listeners in all, is a woman who has had a lot to drink. This drunkenness, one suspects, is habitual for her. She's talking at various people, and she's merry, but she seems unhappy. She's speaking French, loudly. She might be French. She takes a glance at me and says, in English, suddenly louder, Who are you! Who are you!

As though someone had turned to me with a camera in the dark and triggered its flash.

Who are you! she says.

26

I give myself up. On a massage table, I'm vulnerable, as I am in the barber's chair, or during a medical exam, or even when I am at a tailor's being measured for clothes: these moments when the self becomes, primarily, a body. The masseuse is gentle and kind, and as we begin, she says, Do you do a sport? You have a really great body. She says it frankly and clinically but softly. There's no suggestion of blurred boundaries. No, I don't, I say, I don't have a sport, but I know I ought to. I'm getting older, I say, I ought to exercise more. Well, you have an athlete's body, she says.

She doesn't talk much after that. At the end of the session, she says, and this time in a harsher tone, You have a great body, but your back is tight with stress and your neck is full of knots.

My pride is a bit wounded. I'm as offended as I was flattered forty-five minutes earlier.

From time to time, walking down these streets in my dark fedora and loose jacket, a Black woman (it is always a Black woman) will look at me with real recognition; she'll look me in the eye and smile — sometimes a bit puzzled, as though to say, "Who are you?" — and suddenly I'll realize, I really am here.

We who live in these bodies.

27

They take me to Galt, a fine restaurant on Frognerveien. The city is rich, but if you're with people, also convivial. I'm with Andreas and others. By quite a staggering coincidence, Andreas is there as well, dining at the table next to ours.

Cities are made of people: Cathrine, Lene, Åshild, Linn, Linn, Nils, Sofie, Lars, Amund, Johanne, Victoria, Jørgen, Nina, Nadifa, Valeria, Paul, Claudio, Anne-Hilde, Andreas, Andreas, Andreas, Andreas.

28

I talk to Andreas about the quite serious Norwegian enthusiasm for electric cars. Owners of electric cars gain special privileges, he tells me. They can drive in the fast lane, they pay much less in taxes. Electric cars are all the rage in Oslo, he says, and nowhere in the world are as many Teslas sold per capita. Meanwhile, there's all this oil money, there's the staggering wealth of the Government Pension Fund Global, a trillion dollars. We were not imperialists, he says, but there's this weapons trade, hundreds of millions of dollars' worth.

War machines in the morning, and in the evening the Nobel Peace Prize.

Hypocrisy is common to all societies. But is it true, can it be true, that in some places, it is more skillfully hidden than in others?

29

Did you know that there are goats on Utøya Island? In so many ways, life keeps on going.

30

Each culture represents specific instances of sensitivity. This sensitivity is keyed to the needs of mastering the environment, and this accumulated knowledge can quite easily be lost, depending on the challenges proposed by the environment and the easing of such challenges. In times past, an awareness of the clouds on any given day, a knowledge of the behaviors of whales, an intimacy with the patterns of bird migration, an expertise in the varieties of ocean currents, a skill at charting the motions of the sun and other planetary bodies, and a reading of the numerous winds all underpinned the navigational success of the Vikings. These practices of quiet attention were counterweighted to the obvious brutalities.

31

I lower the shutters. The city below. I am in my bed in the apartment given to me in the Litteraturhuset. Night falls after a restless and talkative day. This new fashion among young women in Oslo of not wearing bras. Night falls and I am in my bed in the

Litteraturhuset and I begin to touch myself, in the bed of J. M. Coetzee, Patti Smith, Tomas Tranströmer, Haruki Murakami, Siri Hustvedt, Alain Mabanckou, Ngugi wa Thiong'o, Han Kang, and Arundhati Roy.

We who live in these bodies.

32

Clouds, whales, birds, currents, astronomy, winds. I try to pay attention. Look past the money, past the assurances of prosperity. On July 22, on August 31, on September 2. Everything human is here, and there is nothing here that is not human. I ought to say plainly that I feel the sadness of the city, a sadness all the more powerful because everything around suggests that there is nothing to be sad about.

33

We begin with Lutosławski, and then there's Janáček, and after Janáček comes Schubert. It's as though the music were slowly assembling itself back from fragments, moving back in time, reconstituting until finally we are in the ineffably coherent *Andante con moto* of the String Quartet No. 14 in D minor, D.810. The *Andante con moto* is a set of variations on the theme of the lied "Death and the Maiden." It unfurls at Schubert's heavenly length, which abolishes time.

This is in the Aula of the University of Oslo. Each locale has its pasts, and the Aula's past contains the Nazis and their Norwegian helpers. The hall was used to imprison prisoners of war. The fire in 1943. The Norwegian resistance. It contains, too, Charles Mingus. Thelonious Monk in 1966. And the paintings, eleven of them, by Munch, commissioned in 1914 and delivered in 1916, monumental paintings of *The Sun, History, Alma Mater*. We are all contemporaries and time does not exist. The Munch paintings shine down on us. The Hagen Quartet fills the room with lines of music, and I'm reminded of what Tranströmer wrote in his poem "Schubertiana":

> But those whose eyes enviously follow men of action,
>   who secretly despise themselves for not being murderers,
> don't recognise themselves here,
> and the many who buy and sell people and believe that
>   everyone can be bought, don't recognise themselves here.
> Not their music. The long melody that remains itself in all
>   its transformations . . .

The music enters us. The people of the city, and their foreign guest.

On Carrying and
Being Carried

Every work of translation carries a text into the literature of another language. Fortunate to have had my work translated into many languages, I now exist as an author in the literature of each of those languages. Dany Laferrière, in his 2008 novel *I Am a Japanese Writer*, expresses this slightly strange notion more beautifully than I can:

> When, years later I myself became a writer and was asked, "Are you a Haitian writer, a Caribbean writer or a Francophone writer?" I would always answer that I took the nationality of my reader, which means that when a Japanese reader reads my books, I immediately became a Japanese writer.

Much is found in translation. There's the extraordinary pleasure of having readers in languages one doesn't know. But there's also the way translation makes visible some new aspect of the original text, some influence one absorbs without realizing it. When I think about the Italian translation of my work, I can feel the presence of Italo Calvino and Primo Levi, and I am unnerved and delighted that I mysteriously now share their readership in their language. When I'm translated into Turkish, it is Nâzım Hikmet's political melancholy I think of. Maybe those who like his work will, reading me in Turkish, find something to like in mine as well? In German, perhaps even more than English, I sense the hovering presences of writers who shaped my sensibility—writers like Walter Benjamin, Thomas Mann, Hermann Broch, and W. G. Sebald, among many others. Thanks to translation, I become a German writer.

I trust my translators utterly. Their task is to take my work to a new cohort of my true readers, the same way translation makes me a true reader of Wisława Szymborska, even though I know no Polish, and of Svetlana Alexievich, even though I know no Russian. Gioia Guerzoni, who has translated four of my books into Italian so far, has worked hard to bring my prose into a polished but idiomatic Italian. In 2018, she translated "The Blackness of the Panther." It wasn't an easy text to translate. In particular, the word "Blackness" in the title was a challenge. To translate that word, Gioia considered *nerezza* or *negritudine*, both of which suggest "negritude." But neither quite evoked the layered effect that "Blackness" had in my original title. She needed a word that was about race but also about the color black. The word she was looking for couldn't be *oscurità* ("darkness"), which went too far in the optical direction, omitting racial connotations. So she invented a word: *nerità*. Thus, the title became: *"La nerità della pantera."* It worked. The word was taken up in reviews, and even adopted by a dictionary. It was a word Italian needed, and it was a word the Italian language—the Italian of Dante and Morante and Ferrante—received through my translator.

Translation, after all, is literary analysis mixed with sympathy, a matter for the brain as well as the heart. My German translator,

Christine Richter-Nilsson, and I discussed the epigraph to *Open City*, the very first line in the book. It reads, in English, "Death is a perfection of the eye." The literal translation, the one Google Translate might serve up, would be something like *"Tod ist eine Perfektion des Auges."* But Christine sensed that this rendering would equate "death" with "perfection of the eye," rather than understanding that death was being proposed as the route to a kind of visionary fullness. So she first thought of *"Vollendung,"* which describes a finished state of fullness; then she thought further, and landed on *"Vervollkommnung."* *Vervollkommnung* is a noun that embeds the verb *kommen,* and with that verb, the idea that something is changing and coming into a state of perfection. That was the word she needed.

Christine also knew that what I was calling the eye in my epigraph was not a physical organ (*"das Auge"*), it was the faculty of vision itself. But I didn't write "seeing," so *"des Sehens"* would not quite have worked. In conversation with my German editor, she decided on something that evoked both the organ and its ability: *der Blick.* So, after careful consideration, her translation of "Death is a perfection of the eye" was *"Der Tod ist eine Vervollkommnung des Blickes."* And that was just the first sentence.

The English word *translation* comes from the Middle English, which originates from the Anglo-French *translater.* That in turn descends from the Latin *translatus: trans,* across or over, and *latus,* which is the past participle of *ferre,* to carry, related to the English word "ferry." The translator, then, is the ferry operator, carrying meaning from words on that shore to words on this shore.

. . .

In the summer of 2019, a young woman from Bonn named Pia Klemp was in the middle of a long-drawn-out legal battle in Italy.

Klemp, a former marine biologist, was accused of aiding illegal immigration. As captain of a converted fishing boat named *Iuventa*, she had, in 2017, rescued vessels carrying migrants, launched from Libya and endangered in the Mediterranean, then ferried their precious human lives to the Italian island of Lampedusa. If the case went to trial, as seemed likely, she and nine others in the humanitarian group she worked with faced enormous fines or even up to twenty years in prison for aiding illegal immigration. (Another young German woman, Carola Rackete, was also arrested in Italy for captaining another rescue boat.) Klemp is unrepentant. She knows that the law is not the highest calling. The question she and her colleagues pose is this: do we believe that the people on those endangered boats on the Mediterranean are human in precisely the same way we are human? When I visited Sicily and watched a boat of rescued people with bewildered faces come to shore, there was only one possible answer to that question. And yet we are surrounded by commentary that tempts us to answer it wrongly, or that makes us think our comfort and convenience are more important than human life.

Because Pia Klemp's labor took place on water, it reminded me of an earlier struggle. In 1943, the Danes received word that the Nazis planned to deport Danish Jews. And so, surreptitiously, at great personal risk, the fishermen of North Zealand began to ferry small groups of Danish Jews across the narrow straits to neutral Sweden. This went on, every day, for three weeks, until more than seven thousand people, the majority of Denmark's Jewish population, had been taken to safety.

In each year of this century, hundreds of people have died on the southern border of the United States. Children are separated from their parents and thrown in cages. In the fall of 2011, I visited No Más Muertes (No More Deaths), a humanitarian organization in Arizona that provides aid to travelers by leaving water, blankets, and canned food at strategic points in the Sonoran Desert. These are activities that the US government has declared illegal. The organization also conducts searches for missing migrants, and often locates the bodies of those who have died of hunger or thirst in the desert. A young geographer named Scott Warren, working with No Más Muertes and other groups, sought to help travelers cross safely. He provided water and, when possible, shelter. For this labor, Warren was arrested and charged with harboring migrants. Although the case against him ended in a mistrial, the US Attorney's office in Arizona sought a retrial. Warren is far from the only No Más Muertes volunteer to have been arrested as part of the government's war on those who offer life-saving help to people who ought to be regarded as our fellow citizens.

Can we draw a link between the intricate and often modest work of writers and translators, and the bold and costly actions of people like Pia Klemp, Carola Rackete, and Scott Warren? Is the work of literature connected to the risks some people undertake to save others? I believe so: acts of language can themselves be acts of courage. Both literature and activism alert us to the arbitrary and essentially conventional nature of borders. I think of Edwidge Danticat's words in her book *Create Dangerously*:

> Somewhere, if not now, then maybe years in the future, a future that we may have yet to dream of, someone may risk his or her life to read us. Somewhere, if not now, then maybe years in the future, we may also save someone's life.

And I think of a friend of mine, a filmmaker and professor from Turkey who signed a letter in 2016 condemning the slaughter of

Kurds by the Turkish state and calling for a cessation of violence. She was one of more than eleven hundred signatories from universities and colleges in Turkey. In response, Recep Tayyip Erdoğan's government initiated investigations of every Turkish signatory, accusing them all of terrorism. Most, my friend included, faced long trials and prison sentences. Many have been fired from their jobs or hounded by progovernment students. Some have already been jailed. After the heartache of a trial, the terrorism charges against my friend were finally dropped.

My friend and the other academics were carrying their fellow citizens. With the stroke of a pen, they attempted to carry them across the desert of indifference, over the waters of persecution. For this, they faced consequences similar to those faced by Pia Klemp and Scott Warren: public disrepute, impoverishment, prison time. My friend found herself in great danger for her stand, and it was her turn to be ferried to greater safety.

· · ·

I am struck by a small terra-cotta sculpture made in the fourth century BCE in Etruria (in what is now central Italy). It depicts two figures, a younger man carrying an older man on his back. It is, in fact, a representation of Aeneas carrying Anchises, his father, out of the burning ruins of Troy. The story, recounted in *The Aeneid*, is part of the origin myth of the Roman people. This little sculpture has tremendous affective charge because almost none of us can imagine having to physically carry our own fathers. Support him, yes, in his old age. Actually carry him on your back, no. Impossible to imagine, except in the most wretched emergency. The little Etruscan object is strikingly similar to a famous vignette from the fresco in the Vatican showing the Fire in the Borgo. That fresco, painted in the early sixteenth century by

Raphael or, more likely, Giulio Romano, also shows a young man bearing an old man on his back.

A few years ago, I came across a photojournalist's image of a pair of refugees. I couldn't identify the photographer, but one of the men in the picture is named in the caption as Dakhil Naso. The man he is carrying is his father. They are Yazidis, in flight on foot from ISIS, on their way to Kurdistan. They've been on the move for days, and all you can see behind them is desert. It is a piteous sight: the old man, dressed in white, is on the verge of exhaustion, and the young man, wearing a red football jersey, hardly looks stronger. How far have they come already? How much farther do they have to travel? Why have we allowed this to happen to our fellow citizens?

We all live and die under essentially similar sovereign arrangements, are all subject to the same international banking system, the same alliances among rich nations. We are all citizens under these inescapable powers, but not all of us have our rights of citizenship recognized.

. . .

How can literature help us here? The claim is often made that people who read literature are wiser or kinder, that literature inspires empathy. But is that true? I find that literature doesn't really do those things. After observing the foreign policies of the so-called developed countries, I cannot trust any complacent claims about the power of literature to inspire empathy. Sometimes, even, it seems that the more libraries we have over here, the more likely we are to bomb people over there.

What we can go to literature for is both larger and smaller than any cliché about how it makes us more empathetic. Literature does not stop the persecution of humans or the prosecution of humanitarians. It does not stop bombs. It does not, no matter how finely wrought, change the minds of the fascists who once more threaten to overrun the world. So what is it good for—all this effort, this labor, this sweating over the right word, the correct translation?

I offer this: literature can save a life. Just one life at a time. Perhaps at 4 a.m. when you get out of bed and pull a book of poetry from the shelf. Perhaps over a week in summer when you're absorbed in reading a great novel. Something deeply personal happens there, something both tonic and sustaining.

When I describe literature's effect in these terms, I speak stubbornly in the singular. But I also know I am not alone in the world, and that none of us is. In a speech Albert Camus gave in Uppsala, Sweden, in 1957, he described the collective value of our seemingly disconnected lives:

> Some will say that this hope lies in a nation; others, in a man. I believe rather that it is awakened, revived, nourished by millions of solitary individuals whose deeds and works every day negate frontiers and the crudest implications of history.

And this ever-expanding power of a single life brings to mind a thought that has echoed through the ages. We find it, for instance, in a codex of the Mishnah written in Parma in the mid-thirteenth century: "Whoever destroys a single life is considered by Scripture to have destroyed the whole world, and whoever saves a single life is considered by Scripture to have saved the whole world." Exactly the same thought is expressed in Surah 5 of the Qur'an.

Contrary to the general noise of the culture around us, writing has reminded me in some modest but essential way of things that people don't want to be reminded of. Inside this modest thing called literature, I have found reminders to myself to negate frontiers and carry others across, and reminders of others who carry me, too. Imagine being in an emergency: a house on fire, a sinking boat, a court case, an endless trek, a changed planet. In such an emergency, you can no longer think only of yourself. You have to carry someone else, you have to be carried by someone else.

EPILOGUE

Black Paper

In those days, when portable printers were not so easily available as now, we used to place a single sheet of black paper between two sheets of white. The black paper was carbon paper, crinkly and thin, with a dull shine on one side and a powdery surface on the other. Writing on the top white sheet would transfer the carbon from the black paper onto the bottom white sheet. Black transported the meaning.

In Lahore, I met a man with a sack of crows. The crows were black with pale gray collars, and the sack was a kind of white netting with an inflexible round base. I made a wish and paid the man 150 Pakistani rupees. The man reached into the sack, took out one crow, and let it go.

A blind man was helped through the security checkpoint at Logan.

"The sorry business" refers to mortuary rituals performed by indigenous Australians in the immediate aftermath of a death.

On the train back into Zürich, a group of five young people in their late twenties. Two couples, and one spare. The spare looked longingly at one of the boys. The boy's girlfriend didn't notice, the boy, terribly handsome, didn't notice, but I noticed and the spare noticed that I noticed, they got off the train not long after, swallowed up by the night. That girl's soft sadness, her longing, the things that cannot be said, the cold river flowing past, the empty room, writing this in darkness.

Burned stump of a tree.

Many fell ill, illnesses that showed on the face and illnesses that didn't. We knew, and we didn't know. Poverty began to burrow into those lives. Shame made a home in some people, some went hungry, hunger hollowed them out. The stock market was up, but many pockets were empty.

I was being hunted by a band of men. They were large men, some of them familiar to me. Others had an animal aspect. There was fur, there were feathers and claws and beaks. I ran as harried as any small mammal in the field. Many of the men were bearded, some were masked. Finally they surrounded me and began to beat me. I fought back and I begged. And then one of the men held me in a grip both crushing and caressing. I was sick with mortal fear and disgust. The man smiled, and turned me around, and pushed me down.

The streets of Istanbul were wrapped in beautiful fog, thickening steadily as the morning wore on, coming in in gusts like white smoke, but the fog could not disguise the unhappiness and apocalyptic terror of recent events.

I arrived in Lahore in the early morning, around 4:30, and there was a man there to meet me, some kind of functionary, who guided me through immigration and customs. Then through the darkened streets, and I was at the guest house by 5:30. Unable to sleep, I stayed up until breakfast, served downstairs by serious young men, then came back and swallowed three milligrams of melatonin. When I woke up, I heard that there had been a bombing five miles away. Eight people had died.

When you used the carbon paper correctly, you ended up with two copies of the same document. The top white sheet bore original ink handwriting, the bottom white sheet was the mimic of every stroke and dot. What I had not noted at the time was that on the black paper there was a third copy of whatever had been written. The black paper was ridged and marked with all the original handwriting. Black on black, full of meaning, but shaped by absence. The black paper was the ghostly record. Black on black, secretly sensible.

I dreamed of a bare riverbank, a darkening sky. It wasn't a dream. I was there, on the Missouri River, Doniphan County, Kansas, during the eclipse of the sun. The date was August 21, 2017, the time 1:19 p.m.

We knew and we didn't know. There were rumors. That's how these things usually are. How much did we know exactly? The lights came on in the cities at night. There was the usual clinking of forks on plates in the restaurants, the murmur and din of conversation. Everything was intact, as in any open city harboring an enemy. At the same time, people were thrown in prison for minor offenses. Others lost their livelihoods, arriving in towns that had vanished by the time they got there. Some died on the border. Some cursed God. Some of the trees in the forest volunteered their own branches to serve as ax handles. Invisible faces, swallowed up by the dark. We knew and didn't know.

In Amsterdam I saw the burned paper. It was in a room in a museum piled high with black paper, with burned paper, the work of Daisuke Yokota. But it was not burned paper: it was a pile of crumpled photographs of burned paper. The paper that had been burned and photographed was not blank. Daisuke had taken and printed photographs and then burned them, and had photographed the result.

She wrote to me: I'm sorry, but I have bad news. Our dear John has died.

You cannot reason with a nightmare. The nightmare is the absence of reason. You cannot argue with a nightmare, you can only wake up from one, or wait for it to end.

Out on the riverbank, the totality begins to approach very fast. You notice that your body, like that of an animal under threat, is globally aware of its vulnerability. The brain knows it, the skin knows it, the nerves know it, your legs know it, your back knows it. Your heart reacts, your lungs, your stomach.

What made these dreams strange was not their negative atmosphere but rather the fact that they were nothing but atmosphere.

I remembered none of the actual details, except one: that, during the dream, I had been aware of observing those details in the certainty that, when I woke up, I would remember none of them.

The dream was like something that had burned itself out and left me covered in its ashes. But they were not ashes, since ashes would bring to mind something light and powdery. What I was covered in was the mood of the dream, which was like a dark gray color poured over me, a very dark gray, almost at the point of being black.

How much did we know exactly, at the time it was happening? Some will remember a news report about the fashion designer who made the dresses for the leader's wife. Some might recall a feature about pets, or the absence of pets, at the leader's official residence. These are some of the stories that were told. As for the other stuff, the darker stuff, we knew and didn't know. They said that in the foreign wars, the "rules of engagement" had been "loosened." Certain bodies went uncounted, certain people killed and rotting under rubble.

An incalculable number of people cried themselves to sleep in those days.

Among the piles of photographs of burned photographs was the infinite memory of photography, burned paper, rephotography, and the resulting black paper. It was not a dream. But the next morning, looking at the photograph I had made of Daisuke's work, I began to feel as though I was seeing the things one sees in dreams.

"If they don't see happiness in the picture, at least they'll see the black."

The dark figure. The sorry business.

Navajo people stay inside their homes during the eclipse. Afterward, they say, "In beauty it is finished."

Acknowledgments

The invitation to deliver the Randy L. and Melvin R. Berlin Family Lectures at the University of Chicago in the Spring of 2019 occasioned three of the essays in this book, and also led to the publication of the book itself. I am grateful to the Berlin family for their generosity, and to the organizers of the series for making my time in Chicago so positively memorable.

Black Paper was the work of many hands, and seeing in the dark is a collaborative project. I'm grateful to my editor at the University of Chicago Press, Alan Thomas, and my studio manager and research assistant, Kathy Rong Zhou. In addition, I'd like to thank the following individuals: Jin Auh, Tracy Bohan, Andrew Wylie, Randolph Petilos, Joel Score, Beth Adams, Amitava Kumar, Jake Silverstein, Kathy Ryan, Adedayo Odusina, Alessandra Coppola, Gioia Guerzoni, Amitava Kumar, the late Bisi Silva, the late Okwui Enwezor, Mariam Said, Mena Mark Hanna, Raja Shehadeh, Anna Jäger, Didem Pekün, Joshua Chuang, Susan Meiselas, Kerry James Marshall, Lucas Zwirner, Beth Gordon, Lorna Simpson, Siddhartha Mitter, Matt Seaton, Lucy McKeon, Matt Higginson, Emmanuel Iduma, Mimosa Shah, Nilanjana

Bhattacharjya, Hilary Chidi, Anjali Pinto, Josh Honn, Bethany Hindmarsh, Christine Richter-Nilsson, Josh Begley, Adrienne Edwards, Laura Letinsky, Will Boast, Matthew Jesse Jackson, Anne Walters Robertson, Deborah Nelson, Rachel Cohen, Julianna Joyce, Angela Chen, Paige Johnston, Mohsen Mostafavi, Andreas Wiese, Linn Rottem, Andreas Liebe Delsett, Andreas Viestad, Anne Hilde Neset, Cathrine Bakke Bolin, Bernd Scherer, Mathias Zeiske, Veronika Gugel, Liz Johnston, Garnette Cadogan, Ishion Hutchinson, Rowan Ricardo Phillips, and Josh Begley.

I would like to thank the three anonymous readers who reviewed the manuscript for the University of Chicago Press and provided helpful comments. I'm grateful to my siblings and parents for their kind and steady support with each project, and to Karen Pereira de Andrade — my discussant, partner, and friend — for the beautiful ongoingness of our life journey together.

This book is dedicated to Sasha Weiss, in appreciation of her vigilance, intelligence, sympathy, and presence over the years.

• • •

Versions of some the essays in this book have previously appeared in the *New York Times Magazine,* the *New York Review of Books, Brick, Brittle Paper,* and *Medium.* "Shadow Cabinet: on Kerry James Marshall" is modified from an essay published in *Kerry James Marshall: History of Painting* (David Zwirner Books, 2019). "Bats' Ultrasound" from *New Selected Poems* by Les Murray, © 2007, 2012, 2014 by Les Murray, is reprinted by permission of Farrar, Straus and Giroux, all rights reserved; by permission of Margaret Connolly and Associates, NSW, Australia; and by kind permission of Carcanet Press, Manchester, UK. I am grateful for the support of the John Simon Guggenheim Foundation during the period of writing these essays.

Index